Teaching History, Celebrating Nationalism

This book analyses the relationship between history education and nationalism in the context of the dominant structures of collective memory in Poland. Drawing on original qualitative research with history teachers, it explores the ways in which teachers understand the aims of history teaching and how they teach history, with some contesting or negotiating official and hegemonic nationalist memory projects, while others predominantly reproduce or radicalise them. A study of teachers' tendencies to approach history through the prism of nationalism, this study reveals a view of history lessons as a means of instilling national identity in students, as the past is constructed in nationalist terms and no contradiction is identified in viewing history as both an objective science and a 'nationalising' tool. An examination of the means by which a dominant nationalist discourse is reinforced through historical education, *Teaching History, Celebrating Nationalism* will appeal to scholars of sociology and education with interests in nationalism and memory studies.

Krzysztof Jaskułowski is Associate Professor at SWPS University of Social Sciences and Humanities, Poland, and the author of *The Everyday Politics of Migration Crisis in Poland: Between Nationalism, Fear and Empathy*.

Piotr Majewski is Assistant Professor at SWPS University of Social Sciences and Humanities, Poland.

Adrianna Surmiak is Assistant Professor in the Department of Sociology of Morality and General Axiology at the University of Warsaw, Poland.

Teaching History, Celebrating Nationalism
School History Education in Poland

Krzysztof Jaskułowski, Piotr Majewski and Adrianna Surmiak

LONDON AND NEW YORK

First published 2022
by Routledge
2 Park Square, Milton Park, Abingdon, Oxon OX14 4RN

and by Routledge
605 Third Avenue, New York, NY 10158

Routledge is an imprint of the Taylor & Francis Group, an informa business

© 2022 Krzysztof Jaskułowski, Piotr Majewski and Adrianna Surmiak

The right of Krzysztof Jaskułowski, Piotr Majewski and Adrianna Surmiak to be identified as authors of this work has been asserted by them in accordance with sections 77 and 78 of the Copyright, Designs and Patents Act 1988.

All rights reserved. No part of this book may be reprinted or reproduced or utilised in any form or by any electronic, mechanical, or other means, now known or hereafter invented, including photocopying and recording, or in any information storage or retrieval system, without permission in writing from the publishers.

Trademark notice: Product or corporate names may be trademarks or registered trademarks, and are used only for identification and explanation without intent to infringe.

British Library Cataloguing-in-Publication Data
A catalogue record for this book is available from the British Library

Library of Congress Cataloging-in-Publication Data
A catalog record for this book has been requested

ISBN: 978-0-367-46390-8 (hbk)
ISBN: 978-1-032-11316-6 (pbk)
ISBN: 978-1-003-02852-9 (ebk)

DOI: 10.4324/9781003028529

Typeset in Times New Roman
by Apex CoVantage, LLC

In memory of Professor Wojciech Burszta

Contents

	Preface	viii
1	Setting the ground	1
2	Nationalism, collective memory, education	9
3	Teaching history, celebrating nationalism	29
4	Nationalism, but what kind?	42
5	Whose nation? Whose history?	58
6	What next for teaching history?	88
	Index	94

Preface

At a conference in Germany in 2016, two authors of this book discussed our first research results. Our presentation met with disbelief, and we were told that we Polish exoticised teachers by overestimating their nationalism. We were astonished by the commentators' astonishment. After all, a few months earlier, the elections in Poland had been won by the Law and Justice (PiS) party, following a campaign that relied on overtly nationalist and racist slogans. Right-wing politicians stirred moral panic against Muslim refugees by appealing to the language of exclusionary nationalism and racism. Jarosław Kaczyński, the party leader, warned against the parasites allegedly transmitted by the refugees. Another PiS member, Zbigniew Girżyński, claimed that refugees come to Europe to make jihad and that even Muslim children are a deadly threat. Jarosław Gowin, the prospective Minister for Science, dramatically stated that his role as a Polish politician is to prevent anyone ever blowing up a Polish newborn.

The right-wing politicians were accompanied by ring-wing journalists, some Catholic bishops, and the lower clergy, who also spread anti-refugee rhetoric, presenting Muslims as fundamentally different and threatening others, reminiscent of pre-war anti-Semitic stereotypes. Anti-Muslim threads have also emerged in popular culture: a striking example is Polish nationalist hip-hop warning against the Islamisation of Poland. Anti-Islamic rhetoric was not restricted to the right; some liberals and left-wingers also drew on Islamophobic imagery. In the context of this eruption of nationalism and Islamophobic racism, teachers' attitudes do not seem strange or exotic.

The susceptibility of a large part of Polish society to extreme nationalist slogans must have its causes. This book does not address the electoral success of PiS, and we do not seek to explain who voted for the party and why. However, although we focus on school history education, the significance of this book extends beyond history didactics. By concentrating on the teaching of history at school, this book shows that nationalism, including exclusionary nationalism, is not some kind of marginal aberration in Polish society. On the contrary, we argue that nationalism is strongly embedded in one of the core institutions aimed at socialising the young generations. We show that many teachers aim to teach history not so much as an academic discipline as to impose on the pupils a canonical historical narrative focused on the homogeneous Polish nation. In their understanding, school history should primarily have an identitary function: the pupils are to identify themselves with the Polish nation, the beginnings of which are projected into the distant past. By learning the canonical story of the national past, pupils are to 'discover' who they really are. According to this logic, schools do not teach about nationalism but impose nationalism, which is treated as an unquestionable framework for the interpretation of the past. Moreover, it is often an exclusionary, uncritical, and militant nationalism. Thus, this book constitutes a contribution to the understanding of the nature of nationalism in Poland and, above all, to the comprehension of one of the mechanisms of its institutional production and reproduction.

Acknowledgements

This work was supported by the National Science Centre (grant number UMO-2012/06/A/HS3/00266, UMO-2019/33/B/HS6/00124).

Wrocław – Warszawa, 2019–2021
Krzysztof Jaskułowski, Piotr Majewski,
and Adrianna Surmiak

1 Setting the ground

Memory, nationalism, and school history

Modernity has traditionally been associated with the enlightenment-driven notion of the past as something that is unnecessary and stands in the way of progress. The past was doomed to be a thing of the past. However, the past's significance to modern societies is not diminishing. On the contrary, we have seen an increase in its importance and interest for the last several decades (Shils, 1981; Szacki, 2011). The past has not disappeared into the past, but it is still here in the present and seems to have a long future. Researchers have even written about the 'memory boom', an obsessive interest in memory, tradition, and heritage, which is reflected in the popularity of historical reenactments, the heritage industry, various forms of memorytaintment, such as movies, video games, and series, as well as the social resonance of populist and nationalist ideologies referring to nostalgia for the 'golden age' (Lässig, 2009; Lowenthal, 1998; Nora, 1998; Wineburg, 2018). In the book, we focus on schools, which, despite the domination of popular culture, are still one of the main channels for conveying knowledge about the past. For this reason, school education is also the subject of various historical wars, that is, disputes about the aims and contents of school history. These questions are of particular importance in Poland in the context of the memory politics of the current nationalist government.

Historical education has traditionally been subordinated to nationalist aims in Poland. In line with the official educational policy, school history was intended not so much to teach history as a discipline as to turn pupils into dedicated members of the nation. This book focuses less on top–down politics and institutions such as the Ministry of National Education and more on what is actually taking place in schools themselves. Our aim is to analyse teachers' views on the role of history teaching in the context of the dominant structures of collective memory. We are interested in how teachers themselves perceive the aims of school history education and how they see

DOI: 10.4324/9781003028529-1

cognitive and identity goals. What role do they assign to the formation of national identity in history teaching compared with other identities, such as supranationalism, class, gender, or ethnicity? We explore the question of how teachers view official nationalist educational goals and to what extent they modify or contest them. We are also interested in the type of nationalism that teachers represent and, therefore, how teachers understand the very concept of a nation, how they see Polish national identity, how they perceive obligations towards a nation, and how they see relationships between nations. Finally, our research also includes an analysis of the way in which teachers' views on the goals of education translate into the teaching of history in the context of the representation of selected underprivileged groups.

Why teachers?

Research on historical education has usually focused on two issues. Firstly, studies have zoomed on in students. For example, they have analysed the development of cognitive abilities of students of different ages, the stages of their historical knowledge development, and the understanding of abstract historical concepts, such as change or causality (Lee, 2004). They have also explored how students understand the meaning of specific historical processes and events, for example, the Cold War (Christophe, Gautschi, & Thorp, 2019). In the context of this book, the research by Mario Carretero (2011) is of particular interest. He analysed the way in which patriotic rituals are perceived by students in Argentinean schools, indicating that they reinforce the mythical understanding of the nation as a timeless ontological category, which makes it difficult for pupils to comprehend the concept of historical change.

The second current of research has concentrated on the curriculum, textbooks, and other historical educational media, such as documentaries or historical magazines (Lässig, 2009; Thorp, 2016, 2017). Particular attention has been paid to the study of the core curriculum and textbooks (Hutchins, 2016; Valentin & Van Nieuwehuyse, 2018). As Peter Seixas (2018, p. 282) noted, 'history textbook research comprises the largest single body of research on state-sponsored history in schools'. Textbook research is dominated by content analysis: exploration of the way in which selected historical processes or historical figures are presented, or research on more abstract issues, such as understanding the nation (Christophe et al., 2019; Hutchins, 2011, 2016). These studies have shown that textbooks generally tend to be conservative and resistant to change and often reflect and strengthen the mainstream historical culture in a given society and the dominant structures of collective memory (Foster, 2012; Thorp, 2016). This research trend also is strong in Poland, which is exemplified by studies on the ways of representing national minorities, women, and non-European cultures in textbooks. These analyses have shown that textbooks generally convey a Eurocentric vision of the world, a homogeneous and patriarchal concept of the Polish nation that leaves little space for cultural diversity and ignores the role of women in history (Ambrosewicz-Jacobs & Szuchta, 2014; Chmura-Rutkowska, Głowacka-Sobiech, & Skórzyńska, 2015; Kamusella, 2010; Kowalski, 2008).

Research on historical education both in Poland and in other countries has devoted much less attention to teachers. The few exceptions include Robert Thorp's studies (2016, 2017) on teaching about the Cold War, research on the epistemological views of pre-service teachers (Vinterek, Donnelly, & Thorp, 2017), teachers' use of primary sources (Van Nieuwenhuyse, Roose, Wils, Depaepe, & Verschaffel, 2017; Wansink, Akkerman, Vermunt, Haenen, & Wubbels, 2017), and our own analysis of teachers' views on the relationship between history teaching and nationalism (Burszta et al., 2019; Jaskulowski & Majewski, 2020; Jaskulowski & Surmiak, 2017; Jaskulowski, Majewski, & Surmiak, 2018). However, there are still relatively a small number of studies dealing with teachers whose role has been underestimated in school history-related research, although teachers are among the most important agents responsible for the distribution of historical knowledge in society.

In an era dominated by popular culture, the claim about the major role of teachers in passing on knowledge about the past may seem exaggerated. Many authors have emphasised that the main channel for spreading historical knowledge is popular media (Wineburg, 2018). However, our pilot quantitative studies based on a representative sample of Polish pupils showed that, for the majority of them, history lessons are still the main source of knowledge about the past: 68% of students replied that they learn about the past from history lessons (in comparison, only 2.8% indicated media as the source of their historical knowledge). The majority of students, specifically 79%, also recognised their teacher as an authority on historical issues (Burszta et al., 2019). Of course, it should be remembered that these are only the pupils' declarations and that our research did not address the question of what they understand by historical knowledge. Nevertheless, the results suggest that pupils attribute great importance to history lessons and to teachers as the primary sources of their knowledge about the past.

Polish teachers must follow the core curriculum established by the Ministry of National Education, but the curriculum only sets general objectives and leaves some freedom to teachers, who are responsible for its implementation. They choose textbooks from a list approved by the Ministry, develop syllabuses, and organise the course of lessons. During the lessons, they can use additional materials, highlight certain contents, modify or omit others, and add new ones. It is difficult to categorise Polish schools as having a 'textbook culture' (Kumar, 1988), in which the role of teachers is confined to repeating a textbook's content. Although Polish teachers do not function in a vacuum, they are constrained by the core curriculum, and they may adopt different attitudes towards the dominant concept of history. Therefore, history teachers must be seen as active 'memory makers' (Kansteiner, 2002, p. 197), whose knowledge, views, and attitudes are crucial to what happens in the classroom and what knowledge of the past is transmitted to pupils.

Line of argumentation

We present our analyses in five chapters. Chapter 2 focuses on theoretical and methodological issues and starts with the presentation of our understanding of nationalism, which constitutes the broadest theoretical framework of our explorations. The research on nationalism in schools is dominated by educational research, and we write this book not so much as history didacticians but as sociologists and anthropologists of a nation interested in schools as a state institution that produces and reproduces nationalism (Hutchins, 2016). In clarifying our approach, we discuss the various concepts of nationalism, placing ourselves in a constructivist theoretical camp that focuses on the everyday reproduction of nationalism. However, we argue that analyses of everyday nationalism must take into account the broader context of hegemonic imagery. The chapter also examines the relationship between nationalism and collective memory, focusing on the role of historical education in constructing hegemonic structures of collective memory. Drawing on the literature, we present three ideal types of historical education (nationalist, civic, and disciplinary). Further, we present the institutional context of our analyses by discussing the Polish educational system and the place of history teaching within it. As a baseline for further analyses, we discuss the core curriculum and textbooks. Finally, we elucidate the methodological and ethical aspects of our research.

The next three chapters refer to interviews with teachers and concern, respectively, how teachers define the goals of historical education, what types of nationalism teachers stand for, and how they teach history in the context of the representation of selected disadvantaged groups. More specifically, in Chapter 3, we examine teachers' definition of the goals of history education. We argue that, while there are some differences between teachers, they generally see school history as an instrument for nationalising pupils and instilling national identity in them. We also demonstrate that teachers tend to adopt a naive realistic epistemology based on the belief that history contains fully objective and detached knowledge of the past.

At the same time, however, teachers believe that history has ideological functions and serves to reproduce and consolidate pupils' national identity. We show that, for nationalist-minded teachers, there is no contradiction here because they do not consider the nation to be a contingent and historical construct but an ontological foundation of social and historical reality. Teachers situate the nation beyond time and history by giving it the status of an undisputed and self-evident reality. In this chapter, we also analyse the few contesting teachers (opponents) who reject the nationalist model of education and the naive realistic epistemology. The opponents see history as a domain of construction and interpretation and the nation as a politically entangled project related to modernisation and not a permanent social entity given by nature or God.

In Chapter 4, we focus on the different types of nationalism represented by teachers. While the interviewed teachers generally agreed that the aim of historical education is to nationalise students, they also differed in their idea of what this nationalisation is about. We concentrate on four issues that differentiated the teachers. We analyse their definition of the Polish nation in the context of its inclusiveness and exclusiveness. Then, we explore the importance that the teachers attach to the history of Poland and its uniqueness and the extent to which they take into account the wider international context. Next, we consider how teachers define commitment to the nation and thus what kind of loyalty to the nation they teach their pupils. Finally, we examine the extent to which teachers practise uncritical nationalism or a more critical version.

In Chapter 5, we focus on how differences in the understanding of nationalism translate into the teaching of Polish history in the context of the representation of various underprivileged groups. In other words, whose history do teachers actually teach? We start with an analysis of the representation of the non-European world, pointing out the domination of Eurocentric rhetoric in teachers' narratives, which reflect the Orientalist and civilisation clash discourse of school textbooks. Then, we analyse the teachers' views on the representation of selected underprivileged groups: national minorities, women, and lower classes. In this chapter, we deepen the understanding of nationalism reproduced in history lessons by analysing the degree of inclusiveness of Polish history. We examine the extent to which teachers focus on reproducing the dominant textbook narrative, which does not leave much room for unprivileged groups.

The last chapter, Chapter 6, summarises our findings and discusses them in the context of the education reform undertaken by the right-wing government in 2017. Right-wing politicians framed historical education as being in a state of crisis, that is, as not performing any nationalising functions, which motivated them to pursue a reform to strengthen the nationalist model of education. However, our findings indicate that, in contrast to the right-wing rhetoric, the reform was not a rupture but constitutes a radicalisation of the already-existing school practice. This new reform was in line with the views of the teachers whom we defined as radical nationalists, whose position in the educational system was significantly strengthened. Thus, the new reform subordinated historic education even more strongly to nationalist goals at the expense of teaching history as a discipline. We conclude that the new reform institutionalises exclusionary nationalism and reinforces the teaching history model that promotes naive historical thinking; this does not allow the pupils to comprehend what historical knowledge is or what the role of history in society is. For the vast majority of pupils, school is the only place where they can gain knowledge about history as a discipline. Without this knowledge, they will remain naive consumers of historical and memory content who are incapable of assessing its reliability and validity and susceptible to manipulation.

References

Ambrosewicz-Jacobs, J., & Szuchta, R. (2014). The intricacies of education about the holocaust in Poland. Ten years after the Jedwabne debate, what can Polish school students learn Pabout the holocaust in history classes? *Intercultural Education, 25*, 283–299.

Burszta, W. J., Dobrosielski, P., Jaskulowski, K., Majbroda, K., Majewski, P., & Rauszer, M. (2019). *Naród w szkole: Historia i nacjonalizm w polskiej edukacji szkolnej [The nation at school: History and nationalism in Polish school education]*. Gdańsk: Katedra.

Carretero, M. (2011). *Constructing patriotism: Teaching history and memories in global worlds*. Charlotte, NC: Information Age Publishing, Inc.

Chmura-Rutkowska, I., Głowacka-Sobiech, E., & Skórzyńska, I. (Eds.). (2015). *Niegodne historii? O nieobecności i stereotypowych wizerunkach kobiet w świetle podręcznikowej narracji historycznej w gimnazjum [Unworthy of history? On the absence and stereotypical images of women in light of the historical narrative in middle school textbooks]*. Poznań: WN UAM.

Christophe, B., Gautschi, P., & Thorp, R. (Eds.). (2019). *The cold war in the classroom. International perspectives on textbooks and memory practices*. Cham: Palgrave.

Foster, S. (2012). Re-thinking history textbooks in a globalized world. In M. Carretero, M. Asensio, & M. Rodríguez-Moneo (Eds.), *History education and the construction of national identities* (pp. 49–62). Charlotte, NC: Information Age.

Hutchins, R. D. (2011). Heroes and the renegotiation of national identity in American history textbooks: Representations of George Washington and Abraham Lincoln, 1982–2003. *Nations and Nationalism, 17*, 649–668.

Hutchins, R. D. (2016). *Nationalism and history education: Curricula and textbook in the United States and France*. New York: Routledge.

Jaskulowski, K., & Majewski, P. (2020). Politics of memory in Upper Silesian schools: Between Polish homogeneous nationalism and its Silesian discontents. *Memory Studies*, *13*(1), 60–73.

Jaskulowski, K., Majewski, P., & Surmiak, A. (2018). Teaching the nation: History and nationalism in Polish school history education. *British Journal of Sociology of Education*, *39*(1), 77–91.

Jaskulowski, K., & Surmiak, A. (2017). Teaching history, teaching nationalism: A qualitative study of history teachers in a Polish post-industrial town. *Critical Studies in Education*, *58*(1), 36–51.

Kamusella, T. (2010). School history atlases as instruments of nation-state making and maintenance: A remark on the invisibility of ideology in popular education. *Journal of Educational Media, Memory, and Society*, *2*, 113–138.

Kansteiner, W. (2002). Finding meaning in memory: A methodological critique of collective memory studies. *History and Theory*, *41*, 179–197.

Kowalski, E. (2008). Representations of linguistic and ethnocultural diversity in Poland's education policy, national school curricula and textbooks. *Journal of Multilingual and Multicultural Development*, *29*, 364–379.

Kumar, K. (1988). Origins of India's 'textbook culture'. *Comparative Education Review*, *32*(4), 452–464.

Lässig, S. (2009). Textbooks and beyond. Educational media in context(s). *Journal of Educational Media, Memory and Society*, *1*(1), 1–20.

Lee, P. (2004). Understanding history. In P. Seixas (Ed.), *Theorizing historical consciousness* (pp. 129–164). Toronto: Toronto University Press.

Lowenthal, D. (1998). *The heritage crusade and the spoils of history*. Cambridge: Cambridge University Press.

Nora, P. (1998). *Realms of memory* (Vols. 1–3). New York: Columbia University Press.

Seixas, P. (2018). History in schools. In B. Bevernage & N. Wouters (Eds.), *The Palgrave handbook of state-sponsored history after 1945* (pp. 273–288). New York: Palgrave.

Shils, E. (1981). *Tradition*. Chicago: Chicago University Press.

Szacki, J. (2011). *Tradycja: Przegląd problematyki [Tradition: An overview]*. Warsaw: WUW.

Thorp, R. (2016). *Uses of history in history education*. Umeå: Umeå University & Dalarna University.

Thorp, R. (2017). Experiencing, using, and teaching history. Two history teachers' relation to history and education media. *Journal of Educational Media, Memory and Society*, *9*(2), 129–146.

Valentin, J. P., & Van Nieuwehuyse, K. (Eds.). (2018). *The colonial past in history textbooks*. Charlotte, NC: Information Age Publishing.

Van Nieuwenhuyse, K., Roose, H., Wils, K., Depaepe, F., & Verschaffel, L. (2017). Reasoning with and/or about sources? The use of primary sources in Flemish secondary school history education. *Historical Encounters*, *4*(2), 48–70.

Vinterek, M., Donnelly, D., & Thorp, R. (2017). Tell us about your nation's past. Swedish and Australian pre-service history teachers' conceptualisation of their national history. *Yearbook of the International Society for History Didactics, 38,* 51–72.

Wansink, B. G., Akkerman, S. F., Vermunt, J. D., Haenen, J. P., & Wubbels, T. (2017). Epistemological tensions in prospective Dutch history teachers' beliefs about the objectives of secondary education. *Journal of Social Studies Research, 41*(1), 11–24.

Wineburg, S. (2018). *Why learn history (when it's already on your phone)?* Chicago: The University of Chicago Press.

2 Nationalism, collective memory, education

Introduction

This chapter focuses on presenting the theoretical and methodological basis of our research. Firstly, we situate our analyses in the context of the theory of nationalism, explaining our theoretical approach. We draw on the constructivist paradigm, defining nations through the prism of nationalism, which, in turn, is understood as a political discourse imaging social reality as divided into clearly bounded and distinct sovereign entities called nations. Then, we explore the concepts of collective memory as well as the relationship between nationalism, collective memory, and school historical education. While analysing the links between memory and school education, we describe three models of history teaching: nationalist, civic, and disciplinary. To present the broader context of our study, we also discuss the educational system in Poland, with particular stress on the place that history teaching takes in it. We further examine the dominant structures of Polish collective memory, discussing the content of the core curriculum and school textbooks in the context of the concept of the Polish nation. Then, we briefly present the methodological and ethical issues related to conducting interviews with teachers.

Theorising nationalism and collective memory

Nationalism studies have traditionally focused on the processes of nation building. The main discussions have concerned the questions of how and when nations were formed as well as the issue of continuity between nations and previous communities (Jaskulowski, 2019; Özkirimli, 2010; Smith, 1998). Two main positions have been developed in this debate. Modernists have argued that nations have emerged relatively recently and with no necessary connection to pre-modern communities. Nations are the result of modernisation processes such as state building, urbanisation, industrialisation, capitalism, or democratisation (Gellner, 1983; Hobsbawm, 1990; Smith, 1998). For example, Hobsbawm claimed that the emergence of nations was the result of social engineering related to political modernisation. Governments used nationalism as a means of legitimising the modern state and achieving cultural cohesion. He stressed that nations are a radically new phenomenon that is unprecedented in history, a modern project that breaks with pre-modern times. As he briefly puts it, 'Nations do not make states and nationalisms but the other way round' (Hobsbawm, 1990, p. 10).

At the second pole of this debate, there were ethnosymbolists who stressed that nations have a much longer history than modernists claim and that the beginnings of nations should be traced back to pre-modern times (Guibernau & Hutchinson, 2004; Smith, 1986). The main proponent of this position, Smith (1986), argued that nations were formed on the basis of much older ethnic groups. Smith underlined that, although fully fledged nations developed as a result of modernisation processes, they were formed on the basis of prior ethnic cultural traditions. He believed that the emergence of nations was a continuous and gradual process, which did not constitute a radical break with the pre-modern period. On the margins of this discussion, there were a few primordialists who claimed that a nation is something that is almost eternal and quasi-natural (Coakley, 2018; Özkirimli, 2010; Smith, 1998).

Despite the differences between modernists and ethnosymbolists, they shared, to some extent, a similar view of nations. Both focused on macro-analyses of historical and social processes and large social structures, which they saw as lasting and sound sociological entities (Billig, 1995; Edensor, 2002). It can be claimed that they treated nations as Durkheimian social facts, that is to say, as an external reality that puts pressure on the individual. Referring to Lakoff and Johnson (1980), one can argue that their theories are based on an ontological metaphor of a nation as a thing. Both modernists and ethnosymbolists also see nationalism (understood as a movement and ideology) as an attempt to establish a nation state. They are less interested in nationalism in stable, 'fulfilled' nation states. From both perspectives, nationalism becomes a research problem only when the national movement tries to create a nation state, that is, when the existing political order is questioned and its legitimacy is challenged. Thus, as Billig (1995) noted, both modernists and ethnosymbolists show limited interest in the question of how the 'national' nature of established nation states is naturalised and reproduced on a daily basis (Edensor, 2002).

It was the constructivists who proposed to move beyond the discussion on the beginnings of nations and the attempt to find a universal theory explaining the origin of nations (Billig, 1995; Brubaker, 2004; Edensor, 2002). The constructivist approach is our theoretical starting point. However, we do not refer to any particular theory of nationalism. Rather, we take from authors such as Billig (1995), Brubaker (2004), and Hall (2017) certain assumptions that we treat as sensitising concepts (Blumer, 1954). In other words, the conceptual categories discussed here play a guiding role rather than a strictly defining one. Following the aforementioned authors, we assume that nationalism is not so much a cohesive ideology or a political movement seeking to create its own state as a political discourse focused on the category of nation. In accordance with the constructivist approach, we assume that nations are not really existing social groups that have a permanent essence, clear boundaries, and stable and lasting identities (Brubaker, 2004). This does not mean that nations are not real, but highlights that their realities must be understood in processual terms; nations do not exist as solid entities but are constantly produced and reproduced in the course of the everyday interactions on which all social structures are based (Hall, 2017). As Gwyn A. Williams (1982, p. 190) puts it, 'nations are not born; they are made. Nations do not grow like a tree, they are manufactured'.

We assume that the concept of a nation does not involve some 'ontological collectivism' (Wimmer, 2008, p. 981); it refers not to any sociological reality but to a set of practices and discourses that construct social reality as naturally divided into nations. We presume that nationalism is a way of constructing a social reality characterised by four points: (1) the social world is naturally divided into different, real, and distinct nations (nationalist ontology); (2) every individual, to be fully human, must belong to a nation, and the individual is by nature *homo nationalis* (nationalist anthropology); (3) the individual has obligations to the nation, and loyalty to the nation has priority over other collective loyalties, especially in situations of conflicting obligations (nationalist ethics); and (4) the nation is the only rightful source of political power; therefore, the only legitimate form of state is the nation state (nationalist political theory). In other words, nationalist discourse locates the source of individual identity in a nation, which is given priority over other levels of identity, such as class, locality, or gender. A nation is imagined as a sovereign political community with a clear cultural identity (Anderson, 1991; Smith, 1998).

In the light of the constructivist perspective, the category of nation does not refer to any social totality but implies the dynamic process of assigning meaning to social reality, which is the subject of constant production, contestation, and negotiation in everyday life (Hall, 2017). A number of researchers have stressed that minimal research has been conducted into the bottom–up understanding of a nation (Skey, 2011; Strømsø, 2019). Most of the extant research seems to be about top–down nation building. This book, to some extent, combines the two perspectives – top–down and bottom–up (Jaskulowski, 2019). On the one hand, we look at the top–down construction of national identity by state educational institutions, such as the ministry, schools, and state-approved textbooks. On the other hand, we examine the attitude of teachers towards the official and dominant structures of collective memory. We are interested in how they themselves define the objectives of history teaching and what they think about the textbooks' content.

The concept of hegemony is useful in this context: we apply this concept in a non-essentialist and non-reductionist way, without assuming in advance that economic factors are decisive (Laclau & Mouffe, 2001). We presume that some social actors have more power to define social reality than others and are able to impose their construction of reality (Hall, 2017). In this respect, particularly the control of the state apparatus offers great advantages. The nation state is distinguished not only by its monopoly on the legitimate use of violence but also by a large degree of control over symbolic violence. One of the main elements of power in the domain of symbolic violence is the compulsory and universal education that has been used by modern states to homogenise their populations culturally. However, hegemonic power can always meet with resistance from subordinates (Wimmer, 2008). Following the critical media theory, we assume that hegemonic discourse is never stable and is always susceptible to negotiation and contestation in the decoding process (Hall, 1980). In other words, we assume that people have their own agenda and are capable not only of reproducing but also of negotiating and contesting hegemonic meanings according to their interests, needs, or identities.

The theoreticians of nationalism concurrently emphasise that one of the instruments of nation building is the construction of a common collective memory (Gellner, 1983; Hobsbawm, 1983; Smith, 1999). Although the literature on 'collective memory' is increasing, an agreed definition of the term is still lacking (Jaskulowski & Majewski, 2020; Wertsch & Roediger, 2008). There are many difficulties in trying to define the concept of collective memory, including terminological diversity (different authors have used different terms, e.g., tradition, historical memory, collective memory, and cultural memory), the relationship between memory and history, and 'the precise relation of the collective and the individual' (Kansteiner, 2002, p. 185; Szacki, 2011). As Kansteiner (2002) noted, there are two trends in defining the concept of collective memory. Firstly, this concept may refer to socially shared representations of the past. The analysis focuses here on objectified cultural products related to the past, such as monuments, buildings, or textbooks. The second approach focuses on the different practices of memory production and reception. For the purposes of this book, it is also necessary to distinguish between memory and history (Nora, 1996). However, it must be noted that this distinction is analytical in nature and, in fact, the two types of references to the past exist alongside each other. History refers to the study of the past according to academic discipline standards, while the category of collective memory refers to a broader social phenomenon, namely various shared perceptions of the past functioning in society, which do not necessarily originate from professional historians or follow the discipline's methodological rules (Nora, 1996). Collective memory, therefore, is a broader concept that covers, for example, family stories, historical movies, and historical monuments.

Referring to the critical media theory, we combine the two approaches mentioned earlier (memory as a process of reception and memory as an objectified representation), considering memory as a complex process of communication under the conditions of dominant memory structures that at the same time shape and are being shaped by everyday memory practices (Jaskulowski & Majewski, 2020). To paraphrase Marx, it can be said that people make their own collective memory, but they do not make it as they please; they make it not under self-selected circumstances but within memory structures that exist already. The processual approach to memory immunises us from the reification of collective memory and allows us to think of it as something that people do and not some form of social *Ding an Sich*. It justifies moving beyond the analysis of history curricula and history textbooks and focusing on history teachers; this in turn can provide insights into how the dominant, state-sponsored collective memory is implemented in schools. It enables us to see that teachers can modify the hegemonic concepts of collective memory according to their own interests and agendas. Critical media theory reminds us that 'consensus is not intrinsic to meaning, so the mere dissemination of a certain message does not assure its acceptance' (Ryan, 2011, p. 159). As Hall (1980) argued, meaning is never constant; instead, it must be actively decoded and is always open to different interpretations, which do not have to follow the logic of hegemony.

Nationalism, collective memory, and historical education

As we have already noted, school education, especially historical education, plays an important role in nationalist projects of collective memory formation. As Stephane Lévesque (2008, p. 9) puts it briefly, 'public schooling has traditionally been justified for nation-building purposes'. In the process of nation building, governments have used school history to create a common vision of the past that would form the basis of a national identity that unites citizens (Carretero, 2011). Historians have legitimised the nationalist construction of reality by projecting the existence of nations into a distant past and praising the achievements of their own nations. They have constructed and strengthened the conviction that nations are not contingent collectives but communities of destiny that are deeply rooted in history (Berger & Lorenz, 2010; Majewski, 2013). School history lessons were intended to spread and impose this common vision of the past on students. The history lessons in schools aimed to make children French, English, or German by imposing on them a common collective memory and the cultural identity built on it. Paradoxically, nations were supposedly natural, but their existence required constant production and reproduction.

The construction and imposition of this common memory and identity required, at the same time, the elimination of other traditions and cultural differences, for example, regional and linguistic ones that did not fit into the dominant image of the titular nation (Kamusella, 2009). Traditionally, history teaching in schools had a unifying function: it was part of the construction of a common national past and culture, which proved the nation's permanence and distinctiveness. Particular emphasis was placed on political history because, according to 19th-century notions, a fully fledged nation is a social group that, in the past, had its own state or sought to create it (Hobsbawm, 1990). Historical education was supposed to ensure that children had similar ideas about the past, constructed as a common national history. This prosthetic memory (Landsberg, 2004) was meant to replace the various local, ethnic, or class memories. The common vision of the past that was instilled in schools was also intended to inspire national pride and readiness for sacrifice among pupils. Schools aimed to produce loyal citizens of the nation state who owed it their devotion and, on hearing the slogan 'homeland in danger', would not hesitate to kill its 'enemies' (Anderson, 1991; Hobsbawm & Ranger, 1983).

The nationalising function of school history has long been taken for granted, as have the nations themselves. Although the first criticisms of the dominance of nationalism in history education emerged after the First World War, it was only in the 1960s and 1970s that a critical discussion of school history began on a broader scale (Megill, 2008). Criticism of the naive realist epistemology sensitised historians to the socially and politically conditioned nature of historical knowledge. New trends in historiography, for example women's history, micro-history, and people's history, undermined the traditional concept of political national history. The emerging activism of various minorities, decolonisation, and human rights movements contributed to the undermining of national hegemonic narratives (Appleby, Hunt, & Jacob, 1994). The research by Jerome S. Bruner (1960) was also of key importance here. Bruner (1960) initiated a 'cognitive revolution' in education that relied on learning methods of accessing knowledge instead of acquiring ready-made knowledge (Foster, 2012, p. 55; Lévesque, 2008, pp. 10–13). Following this ferment, debates emerged on what history should be taught in schools. Many states, for example the UK, the Netherlands, West Germany, and Belgium, introduced history education reforms that put more stress on teaching pupils how to think as historians than on memorising coherent canonical national history (Megill, 2008; Seixas, 2018; Van Nieuwenhuyse, 2018).

The tendency to move from a model of history as national memory to a disciplinary approach was not unidirectional and irreversible. Reforms often triggered fierce debates and counteractions from conservatives and nationalists, leading to various 'historical wars', for example disputes over textbooks (Macintyre & Clark, 2003; Nash, Crabtree, & Dunn, 1997). The 1990s saw the start of discussions about the Holocaust and the role of school history in shaping attitudes of responsibility and tolerance, which revived the model of history as memory (Seixas, 2018). In summary, drawing on the work of Peter Seixas (2018) and Karel Van Nieuwenhuyse (2018), we distinguish three models of education: nationalist, civic, and disciplinary. These models should not be understood in a chronological sense; they do not follow one direction. It also has to be noted that the boundaries between the models are not always clear. We understand these models as ideal types in the Weberian sense, which serve as a useful analytical framework in which to organise our empirical material (Swedberg, 2018). Real education systems refer to different models simultaneously, for example combining disciplinary and nationalist model elements.

The nationalist model involves subordinating history teaching to the aims of constructing and consolidating a national identity among pupils. The goal of education lies in imposing on students a common and coherent national narrative to form the basis of a common national identity. As Seixas (2018, p. 274) briefly stated, the teaching of history is mostly reduced to 'overtly nationalistic, solidarity-enhancing mythologies'. The cognitive goals are essentially secondary here. The past is a pretext for talking about national imponderables that are treated as a timeless norm. It is in this respect that history resembles mythology: students learn 'sacred' and canonical stories that legitimise the nationalist construction of reality and strengthen the hegemonic concept of national identity (Szacki, 2011). History teaching focuses on selected events that are seen as archetypical and on teaching history by celebrating national heroes presented as moral examples for students to follow. In a word, history teaching takes the form of a pedagogy of national memory.

The civic model focuses on educating critical and informed citizens who appreciate democratic principles. History education is about the promotion of 'universal' civic values, such as engagement, tolerance, responsibility, criticism, and care for the environment. There is a strong emphasis on global education based on the assumption that citizenship and engagement should be transnational and global (Bromley, 2009; Goren & Yemini, 2017). This model has certain features in common with the nationalist one. Similarly to the nationalist model, it largely subordinates cognitive goals to other goals, namely the aim of forming a citizen's identity. Thus, the civic model also tends to turn history into mythology (Van Nieuwenhuyse & Wils, 2012). For example, studies about the Holocaust have often focused on 'the lessons of the Holocaust, and have neglected the big historical question of why and how the Holocaust happened' (Salmons, 2003, p. 140). In other words, this model treats the study of the past as a pretext to convey timeless universal values to pupils. The model places more emphasis than the nationalist model on critical thinking, discussion, and the student's own work. However, the critical thinking in this model has its limits: different particular narratives are criticised, but the universal preferred narrative tends to be excluded from criticism and presented as an objective, uncontested story.

Another model is 'discipline-informed history education' (Seixas, 2018, p. 274). It concentrates on introducing students to the methodology of historical research. The goal here is to teach the basics of history as an academic discipline. This model emerged from the aforementioned debates on education in the 1960s and 1970s. The model in its pure form is a rare occurrence because, as we have noticed, it often meets with opposition from conservatists and nationalists, who see it as a threat to national identity. The core curriculum lessons based on this model 'downplay the uses of history for the present and the connection between history and students' identities' (Seixas, 2018, p. 276). It is not intended to teach a coherent story about the past to serve as a source of national identity or to look at the past as a reservoir of examples confirming the importance of timeless values, whether national or civic. The history lessons are based on active methods aimed at developing the skill of 'thinking like a historian' among students (Mandell & Malone, 2007). For example, students learn to ask historical questions and learn about internal and external source criticism, source analysis, or historical explanation. The aim of teaching history is to develop genetic historical consciousness, that is, to enhance the understanding of how historical knowledge is produced and how it is conditioned and positioned (Rüssen, 2004).

School history education in Poland

History has traditionally played an important role in Polish nationalism. When the first Polish nation state was established in 1918 (in accordance with nationalist teleology, Polish historiography presents it as a rebirth of independence), history became an obligatory school subject (Glimos-Nadgórska, 2015). The teaching of history was based on a nationalist model in line with the assumption that history is the basis of national identity (Kamusella, 2017). This legacy of nationalist memory pedagogy has proved to be very persistent. Even during the communist period, despite the emphasis on social issues and class struggle, the lessons of history were generally subordinated to nationalist logic. Whilst the communists stressed the history of the lower social classes and international working class links, it was still content-related national history. Moreover, to increase their legitimacy, the communists willingly resorted to Polish nationalist rhetoric, which was also reflected in school education (Zaremba, 2001). One of the main elements of this rhetoric was the Piast myth, which presented the medieval Piast state as an antecedent of the modern homogeneous Polish nation state. The textbooks emphasised that, thanks to Polish communists and the alliance with the USSR, Poland returned to its natural borders from the Piast period and again became an ethnically homogeneous state (Górny, 2007; Thum, 2011; Wojdon, 2017a).

During the communist era, a centralised educational system was created, controlled by the communist party, which decided on the content of curricula and textbooks. There was just one party-approved textbook for each grade. The textbooks were rarely updated and were sometimes published in an unchanged form for as long as ten years (Wojdon, 2017b). The fall of communism brought education reforms, including history teaching. In the context of historical education, two major changes were important. Firstly, the new core curriculum was introduced, presenting a new interpretation of history depicting communism not as the apogee of mankind's achievements but as a catastrophe and introducing topics that were silenced during communism, such as the Katyń massacre. The changes were accompanied by the rhetoric of discovering the 'white spots' and 'unlying' history: the 'false' communist narrative was replaced by allegedly 'true' history. Secondly, the school textbook market was liberalised. Censorship and state monopoly were abolished, but a degree of state control was maintained: for a textbook to be approved for school use, it had to obtain the approval of the Ministry of National Education (Wojdon, 2017b).

Another education reform was conducted by the conservative–liberal coalition government in 1999. The reform changed the structure of the education system inherited from the communist period. It abolished the two-tier school system (eight years of elementary school and four years of secondary school or three years of vocational school) and introduced a three-tier system, which existed at the time of our research. The reform established a compulsory six-year primary school (PS) for children aged 7 to 13 (since 2014, compulsory primary education has started at the age of 6). The next stage of compulsory education was lower secondary school (LSS), which lasted for three years, followed by the part-time compulsory educational stage, in which students had to continue their education until the age of 18 in upper secondary schools (USSs) or through vocational training offered by employers (Polish EURIDICE Unit, 2012). There were two main types of USSs: general upper secondary schools (GUPSs) and various types of vocational upper secondary schools (VUPSs). In this system, history was taught in PSs from the fourth to sixth grade as the subject History and Society, which combined elements of history with civics. History as a distinct subject was taught in LSSs and USSs. At each stage of education, students were taught the entire history course from ancient times to the 20th century but in a progressively more detailed way.

In 2008, the liberal–conservative government implemented another reform by modifying curricula and introducing the option for pupils to choose the subjects in which they wanted to specialise. The reform came into force in 2012 and, in the case of history, involved a partial break from repeating the history course at each stage of education. In PSs, history teaching remained unchanged and covered the period from ancient times to modern times. In LSSs, students had to learn history from ancient times until 1914. In all types of USSs, history was obligatory in the first grade and covered the period from 1914 to the present day. After completing the first grade, the pupils could decide whether they wanted to learn history as a major subject, which ended with an exam in the last grade. If they chose this option, they learned history from ancient times to modern times but on a more detailed level. Pupils who did not choose history as a major subject but decided, for example, to focus on physical sciences had to study a compulsory subject, 'History and Society'. This subject consisted of thematic modules focused on some historical periods, processes, or issues (e.g. early modern history, family history, and media history) (Polish EURIDICE Unit, 2012).

The way in which the reform was introduced and the lack of consultation provoked criticism from various educational milieus. Right-wing journalists and politicians also joined in the criticism, transforming the debate into a history war. The right-wingers considered the replacement of the classic history lessons with the subject 'History and Society' as a dangerous attempt to drive history out of school. They warned that pupils would leave school without knowing the canonical story of Poland's past, which could erode their national identity. As a result, they cautioned, the existence of the Polish nation was threatened. Under the influence of this criticism, the government modified its plans and decided that, within the subject 'History and Society', there would be a compulsory module, 'National Pantheon and National Disputes', devoted mainly to the political and military history of Poland and subordinated to the goal of consolidating the pupils' national identity (Wojdon, 2019). Although the right wing criticised the government for its alleged plans to weaken the Polish national identity, the government reform largely maintained a nationalist model of historical education. The comments published alongside the new core curriculum accompanying the 2008 reform by the Ministry of National Education stated that:

> In Poland, history teaching has always played a special role – historical knowledge is considered to be the glue of the national and civilisation – cultural community. . . . It should not only introduce pupils to the heritage of past eras, but also shape their attitudes – introduce them to the general human value system, instil values associated with tradition, especially homeland tradition, strengthen their attachment to the idea of freedom and tolerance, prepare them to participate in public life. . . . The aim of historical education . . . is also to get students familiar with the historian's workshop and shape the so-called historical thinking and skills allowing for creative and active participation in the learning process.
>
> (MEN, 2012, p. 67)

The commentary echoes the discussion on the need to teach history as a discipline and to include active teaching methods. However, as Joanna Wojdon (2017b, p. 161) noted, 'these ideas are not reflected in the main body of the curriculum'. The quoted excerpt may suggest that the core curriculum puts emphasis on shaping different values and that national values have no priority. Similarly, the main body of the curriculum itself speaks of different values and loyalties. For example, the primary school curriculum mentions the formation of civic participation, social sensitivity, tolerance, and ties with groups of different scales: 'the pupil feels a bond with the local, national, European and global community' (MEN, 2012, p. 34). However, the core curriculum actually focuses on teaching the history of the Polish nation, which is presented as the main object of loyalty. For example, the subject 'History and Society' for PSs covers 17 historical topics, 10 of which are devoted to Polish history. The remaining topics concern civics and teach that the supreme form of loyalty for the human being is the nation state. As another example, the core curriculum for the first grade of PSs is dominated by 'political history (about 80%), with a prevalence of national history content, with a strong synchronisation of Polish history with European and world history' – as we read in the official commentary (MEN, 2012, p. 9). Thus, out of 17 thematic blocks, 12 concern exclusively Polish history and the remaining 5 are devoted to general history, but they also contain Polish themes.

The core curriculum provides only a general framework and leaves some room for teachers themselves to decide how they will implement it and which topics they will teach. Some teachers even admitted in interviews that they do not know the core curriculum well. This was partly due to the fact that the teachers were exhausted, as they put it, by constant educational reforms and the accompanying training, workshops, and reorganisations and did not pay much attention to official documents, fearing that things would change again soon anyway. Some teachers, however, felt that they themselves know what is important and what is not and what they should teach their pupils. As we mentioned, the teachers also decide themselves which textbook to use provided that it is on the list accepted by the Ministry of National Education. Since the liberalisation of the publishing market, numerous history textbooks have been published. However, quantitative studies on a representative sample of teachers have shown that the textbooks from the three main publishers have monopolised the market (Burszta et al., 2019).

The Ministry of National Education appoints reviewers to evaluate the textbooks and verify their compatibility with the core curriculum (Wojdon, 2017b). Publishers, therefore, adapt the textbooks to the core curriculum. As a result, textbooks 'follow the recommendations of the curriculum regarding the sequence of issues discussed and therefore their tables of content are almost identical' (Wojdon, 2017b, p. 162). The textbooks are aimed at conveying content and teaching facts, an approach that 'is deeply rooted in the Polish tradition of teaching history' (Wojdon, 2017b, p. 167). They devote marginal attention to developing historical thinking and research skills. All the textbooks use 'a traditional framework of the dominating authors' narrative' (Wojdon, 2017b, p. 162). They do not discuss controversial issues, such as the scale of Poles' participation in the Holocaust or Polish colonial plans (Balogun, 2018; Dobrosielski, 2017). As Wojdon wrote, 'the Polish textbooks generally tend not to bother pupils with historians' dilemmas. The reconstructionist paradigm absolutely dominates. Readers are expected to read, understand and memorise the information. . . . Even if contradictory opinions are presented, "the better" one is chosen by the author or is to be chosen by pupils' (Wojdon, 2017b, p. 165). As she summarised, the core curriculum and textbooks go in line with 'the national collective memory paradigm of school history' (Wojdon, 2017b, p. 171).

Contrary to right-wing claims, the reform has not changed the model of historical education aimed at producing and consolidating a national identity based on a homogeneous concept of the Polish nation. Traditionally, Polish historical education defined the Polish nation as culturally uniform, as demonstrated by research on the representation of national minorities in textbooks (Ambrosewicz-Jacobs & Szuchta, 2014; Burszta et al., 2019; Kamusella, 2010; Kowalski, 2008). It should be stressed that the question of national minorities is an important theme in the context of Polish history. For most of its history, Poland was inhabited by various ethnic, linguistic, religious, and national groups, the most numerous of which were Belarusians, Germans, Jews, and Ukrainians. In the interwar period, for example, national minorities made up almost a third of the population. Poland was populated, among others, by over three million Jews, who accounted for around 10% of the total population. It was only in the aftermath of the Second World War that Poland became an almost homogeneous nation state, with the Polish language and the Catholic population predominating. Today, Poland is one of the most homogeneous and 'white' societies in Europe. According to various estimates, in contemporary Poland, national and ethnic minorities constitute only 2–3% of the total population. However, in the last decade, Poland has become attractive to migrants, especially from Ukraine and the countries of the former Soviet Union and to a much lesser extent from South Asia (Jaskulowski, 2019; Jaskulowski, Majewski, & Surmiak, 2018).

The creation of an ethnically homogeneous nation state has been the goal of Polish integral nationalism, represented by the National Democracy (ND), since the end of the 19th century. Polish nationalists wanted to assimilate Slavic minorities and exclude others, especially Jews, whom they considered to be radically different culturally and racially. Nationalist ideas had a great influence on the politics of the Polish nation state, especially in the 1930s. For example, they led to various discriminatory educational policies and informal actions towards national minorities, such as closing schools with minority languages or limiting the number of Jewish students at universities (Kamusella, 2009; Porter, 2000). Paradoxically, communist rule has strengthened the domination of a homogeneous concept of the Polish nation. As we have already noted, the communists tried to increase their legitimacy and adopted many elements of traditional nationalist rhetoric and politics (Zaremba, 2001). It was only the political transformation of the 1980s and 1990s that paved the way for a more open policy, including the education policy, towards national minorities (Jaskulowski, 2012; Łodziński, 2005). Against this background, we should read the conclusions from the recent, aforementioned analysis of Polish history textbooks, which speaks to the domination of ethnic concepts of the nation, exclusive of national minorities and cultures (Kowalski, 2008).

The textbooks used by history teachers also fit into this pattern. They not only marginalise national minorities but also present the celebratory, unilinear, and teleological history of a homogeneous Polish nation that is inextricably linked to Catholicism, which allegedly existed in its embryonic form in the early Middle Ages. Referring to Wertsch's (2002) concept of narrative schemas, it can be said that the main protagonist of the textbook narrative is the Polish nation, symbolised mainly in line with the traditional national historiography by male figures belonging to the upper layers of society: kings, leaders, and politicians. The adventures of the Polish nation can be written into a narrative scheme that can be summarised in four points: the Polish nation lives in peace, peace is interrupted by some internal or external threat, there is a time of suffering and united struggle against the odds, and finally the Polish nation triumphs over its enemies, proving its love for independence. The textbooks present this narrative as an uncontested objective single story with which pupils should identify (Jaskulowski et al., 2018).

Researching history teachers

As we have already explained, teachers have some freedom in implementing the core curriculum. Therefore, it cannot be assumed a priori that the goals of historical education as defined in the curriculum are a good guide to school practice. The teachers' attitudes are also crucial here, and we decided to explore them through semi-structured interviews (Brinkmann & Kvale, 2018). The choice of method was dictated by two considerations. Firstly, our interviewees proved to be difficult to access due to their tight schedule. Many teachers worked in several schools or worked overtime. It was difficult to obtain permission to take part in the research. Hence, we knew that we would probably only have one chance to interview a particular teacher, which influenced our choice of method. Secondly, conducting semi-structured interviews is a flexible method that combines closed and open questions. This allowed us to explore the threads that we are interested in while at the same time giving teachers the opportunity to raise topics that are important to them.

We conducted a total of 186 interviews. The number of interviews is unusually high by qualitative research standards. We can, therefore, be sure that saturation has been achieved (Guest, Bunce, & Johnson, 2006). In our sample selection, we also followed the maximising diversity principle; that is, we sought to interview a wide variety of teachers in terms of gender, age, work experience, place of residence, and type of school. We conducted interviews both in metropolitan cities, such as Warsaw, Wrocław, and Katowice, and in medium-sized and small towns, such as Wałbrzych and Brzeg. Some interviews took place in borderland areas inhabited by minorities, for example Upper Silesia. We talked to teachers from all levels of education. Women predominated among the teachers, which reflects the structure of this professional group. The age of the teachers ranged from 30 to 60 years. All the interviewees had higher education, which is a necessary condition for obtaining a job at a school in Poland. The teachers agreed to participate in the research under the condition of anonymity and confidentiality (Surmiak, 2018). Respecting the teachers' wishes, we do not provide any personal data that would allow their identity to be discovered.

All the interviews were recorded and transcribed, and we obtained permission to use them for academic purposes, provided that they were anonymised. Our analysis relied on multiple readings of each transcription and open coding (Saldaña, 2012). To ensure the credibility of our interpretation, we coded the interviews independently and then compared and agreed our interpretations (Strauss & Corbin, 1998). We are aware that we established a concrete agenda by asking teachers about the links between history and nationalism. Teachers could have responded in the way that they thought they should respond by repeating what they had read in the curriculum. This danger could not be completely avoided, but we think it has been mitigated by two factors. Firstly, the core curriculum sets only general principles and leaves a certain amount of autonomy to teachers, and teachers are aware of this. Secondly, we tried not to impose topics and not to ask directly about national issues; instead, our questions focused on textbook evaluation. The teachers could raise any problems related to the textbooks – if they raised nation-related issues, then these issues were explored by the interviewees (Jaskulowski & Surmiak, 2017).

Conclusions

This chapter presented our theoretical framework and outlined the broader historical and institutional context of our analyses. In accordance with the constructivist approach, we defined nationalism as a discursive process of constructing social reality. We demonstrated that nation states have traditionally used school history education to make pupils into devoted and loyal nationals. Although, since the 1960s and 1970s, the nationalist model of historical education has attracted criticism, it still has a dominant position in Poland. The subordination of historical education to nationalist aims in Poland stems from several factors. Firstly, in Poland, there is a strong tradition of defining historical education in nationalist terms. Secondly, this tradition of historical education as national memory stems from the dual role played by historians: they have been both researchers and national ideologists who see themselves as guardians of national identity. Thirdly, there is the domination of the erudite Rankian model of history among historians in Poland, which also finds its expression in the approach to history didactics, the core curriculum, and textbooks. Although there are elements of a disciplinary approach in the core curriculum, both the core curriculum and the textbooks place the main emphasis on detailed content-related knowledge focused on the Polish nation. Pupils are expected to master the canonical story of Polish history, with which they should identify. However, the content of the core curriculum or the textbooks does not say much about school practice. The decisive factor here is the teachers. In line with our constructivist and dynamic approach to the nation and memory, we treat teachers as active memory makers who can not only reproduce dominant ideas but also modify or challenge them according to their identities and interests.

References

Ambrosewicz-Jacobs, J., & Szuchta, R. (2014). The intricacies of education about the holocaust in Poland: Ten years after the Jedwabne debate, what can Polish school students learn about the holocaust in history classes? *Intercultural Education*, *25*, 283–299.

Anderson, B. (1991). *Imagined communities: Reflections on the origin and spread of nationalism*. London: Verso.

Appleby, J., Hunt, L., & Jacob, M. (1994). *Telling the truth about history*. New York: Norton.

Balogun, B. (2018). Polish lebensraum: The colonial ambition to expand on racial terms. *Ethnic and Racial Studies*, *41*, 2561–2579.

Berger, S., & Lorenz, C. (Eds). (2010). *Nationalizing the past: Historians as nation builders in modern Europe*. New York: Palgrave.

Billig, M. (1995). *Banal nationalism*. London: Sage.

Blumer, H. (1954). What is wrong with social theory? *American Sociological Review*, *19*(1), 3–10.

Brinkmann, S., & Kvale, S. (2018). *Doing interviews*. London: Sage.

Bromley, P. (2009). Cosmopolitanism in civic education: Exploring cross-national trends: 1970–2008. *Current Issues in Comparative Education*, *12*, 33–44.

Brubaker, R. (2004). *Ethnicity without groups*. Cambridge, MA: Harvard University Press.

Bruner, J. (1960). *The process of education*. Cambridge, MA: Harvard University Press.

Burszta, W. J., Dobrosielski, P., Jaskulowski, K., Majbroda, K., Majewski, P., & Rauszer, M. (2019). *Naród w szkole: Historia i nacjonalizm w polskiej edukacji szkolnej [The nation at school: History and nationalism in Polish school education]*. Gdańsk: Katedra.

Carretero, M. (2011). *Constructing patriotism: Teaching history and memories in global worlds*. Charlotte, NC: Information Age Publishing, Inc.

Coakley, J. (2018). 'Primordialism' in nationalism studies: Theory or ideology? *Nations and Nationalism*, *24*, 327–347.

Dobrosielski, P. (2017). *Spory o Grossa: Polskie problemy z pamięcią o Żydach [Disputes about Gross: Polish problems with the memory of Jews]*. Warsaw: IBL PAN.

Edensor, T. (2002). *National identity, popular culture and everyday life*. Oxford: Berg.
Foster, S. (2012). Re-thinking history textbooks in a globalized world. In M. Carretero, M. Asensio, & M. Rodríguez-Moneo (Eds.), *History education and the construction of national identities* (pp. 49–62). Charlotte, NC: Information Age.
Gellner, E. (1983). *Nations and nationalism*. Oxford: Blackwell.
Glimos-Nagórska, A. (2015). Miejsce nauczania historii w polskim systemie edukacyjnych w XX wieku [The place of history teaching in the Polish educational system in the 20th century]. *Zeszyty Naukowe Uniwersytetu Jagiellońskiego. Prace Historyczne, 142*(2), 257–279.
Goren, H., & Yemini, M. (2017). Global citizenship education redefined – A systematic review of empirical studies on global citizenship education. *International Journal of Educational Research, 82*, 170–183.
Górny, M. (2007). *Przede wszystkim ma być naród. Marksistowskie historiografie w Europie Środkowo-Wschodniej [First of all there must be a nation. Marxist historiographies in Central Eastern Europe]*. Warszawa: Trio.
Guest, G., Bunce, A., & Johnson, L. (2006). How many interviews are enough? An experiment with data saturation and variability. *Field Methods, 18*(1), 59–82.
Guibernau, M., & Hutchinson, J. (2004). *History and national destiny: Ethnosymbolism and its critics*. Oxford: Blackwell.
Hall, S. (1980). Encoding/decoding. In S. Hall, D. Hobson, A. Lowe, & P. Willis (Eds.), *Culture, media, language* (pp. 128–138). London: Hutchinson.
Hall, S. (2017). *The fateful triangle: Race, ethnicity, nation*. Cambridge, MA: Harvard University Press.
Hobsbawm, E. (1983). The mass-producing traditions, Europe, 1870–1914. In E. Hobsbawm & T. Ranger (Eds.), *The invention of tradition* (pp. 262–307). Cambridge: Cambridge University Press.
Hobsbawm, E. (1990). *Nations and nationalism since 1780: Programme, myth, reality*. Cambridge, MA: Cambridge University Press.
Hobsbawm, E., & Ranger, T. (Eds.). (1983). *The invention of tradition*. Cambridge: Cambridge University Press.
Jaskulowski, K. (2012). *Wspólnota symboliczna [Symbolic community]*. Gdańsk: Katedra.
Jaskulowski, K. (2019). *The everyday politics of migration crisis in Poland: Between nationalism, fear and empathy*. Cham: Palgrave.
Jaskulowski, K., & Majewski, P. (2020). Politics of memory in upper Silesian schools: Between Polish homogeneous nationalism and its Silesian discontents. *Memory Studies, 13*(1), 60–73.
Jaskulowski, K., Majewski, P., & Surmiak, A. (2018). Teaching the nation: History and nationalism in Polish school history education. *British Journal of Sociology of Education, 39*(1), 77–91.
Jaskulowski, K., & Surmiak, A. (2017). Teaching history, teaching nationalism: A qualitative study of history teachers in a Polish post-industrial town. *Critical Studies in Education, 58*(1), 36–51.

Kamusella, T. (2009). *The politics of language and nationalism in modern Central Europe*. London: Palgrave.

Kamusella, T. (2010). School history atlases as instruments of nation-state making and maintenance: A remark on the invisibility of ideology in popular education. *Journal of Educational Media, Memory, and Society, 2*, 113–138.

Kamusella, T. (2017). *The un-Polish Poland, 1989 and the illusion of regained historical continuity*. Cham: Palgrave.

Kansteiner, W. (2002). Finding meaning in memory: A methodological critique of collective memory studies. *History and Theory, 41*(2), 179–197.

Kowalski, E. (2008). Representations of linguistic and ethnocultural diversity in Poland's education policy, national school curricula and textbooks. *Journal of Multilingual and Multicultural Development, 29*, 364–379.

Laclau, E., & Mouffe, C. (2001). *Hegemony and socialist strategy: Towards a radical democratic politics*. London: Verso.

Lakoff, G., & Johnson, M. (1980). *Metaphors we live by*. Chicago: Chicago University Press.

Landsberg, A. (2004). *Prosthetic memory: The transformation of American remembrance in the age of mass culture*. New York: Columbia University Press.

Lévesque, S. (2008). *Thinking historically: Educating students for the twenty-first century*. Toronto: University of Toronto Press.

Łodziński, S. (2005). *Równość i różnica. Mniejszości narodowe w polskim porządku demokratycznym po 1989 roku [Equality and difference. National minorities in Polish democracy after 1989]*. Warsaw: Scholar.

Macintyre, S., & Clark, A. (2003). *The history wars*. Melbourne: Melbourne University Press.

Majewski, P. (2013). *(Re)konstrukcje narodu. Odwieczna Macedonia powstaje w XXI wieku [The reconstruction of the nation: Eternal Macedonia emerging in 21th century]*. Gdańsk: Katedra.

Mandell, N., & Malone, B. (2007). *Thinking like a historian: Rethinking history instruction: A framework to enhance and improve teaching and learning*. Madison: Wisconsin Historical Society Press.

Megill, A. (2008). Historical representations, identity, allegiance. In S. Berger, I. Eriksonas, & A. Mycock (Eds.), *Narrating the nation* (pp. 19–34). New York: Berghahn Books.

MEN. (2012). *Podstawa programowa z komentarzami [Core curriculum with commentary]* (Vol. 4). Warsaw: MEN.

Nash, G. B., Crabtree, C., & Dunn, B. (1997). *History on trial: Culture wars and the teaching of the past*. New York: Knopf.

Nora, P. (1996). General introduction: Between memory and history. In L. Kritzman (Ed.), *Realms of memory: The construction of the French past* (pp. 1–20). New York: Columbia University Press.

Özkirimli, U. (2010). *Theories of nationalism: A critical introduction*. New York: Palgrave.

Polish EURIDICE Unit. (2012). *The system of education in Poland*. Warsaw: Polish EURIDICE Unit.

Porter, B. (2000). *When nationalism began to hate: Imagining modern politics in nineteenth century Poland.* Oxford: Oxford University Press.
Rüssen, J. (2004). Historical consciousness: Narrative structure, moral function and ontogenetic development. In P. Seixas (Ed.), *Theorizing historical consciousness* (pp. 63–85). Toronto: Toronto University Press.
Ryan, L. (2011). Memory, power and resistance: The anatomy of a tripartite relationship. *Memory Studies, 4*(2), 154–169.
Saldaña, J. (2012). *The coding manual for qualitative researchers.* Los Angeles, CA: Sage.
Salmons, P. (2003). Teaching or preaching? The holocaust and intercultural education in the UK. *Intercultural Education, 14*(2), 139–149.
Seixas, P. (2018). History in schools. In B. Bevernage & N. Wouters (Eds.), *The Palgrave handbook of state-sponsored history after 1945* (pp. 273–288). New York: Palgrave.
Skey, M. (2011). *National belonging and everyday life: The significance of nationhood in an uncertain world.* Basingstoke: Palgrave.
Smith, A. D. (1986). *The ethnic origins of nations.* Oxford: Blackwell.
Smith, A. D. (1998). *Nationalism and modernism: A critical survey of recent theories of nations and nationalism.* London and New York: Routledge.
Smith, A. D. (1999). *Myths and memories of the nation.* Oxford: Oxford University Press.
Strauss, A., & Corbin, J. M. (1998). *Basics of qualitative research.* Thousand Oaks, CA: Sage.
Strømsø, M. (2019). 'All people living in Norway could become Norwegian': How ordinary people blur the boundaries of nationhood. *Ethnicities, 16*, 1338–1157.
Surmiak, A. (2018). Confidentiality in qualitative research involving vulnerable participants: Researchers' perspectives. *Forum: Qualitative Social Research, 19*(3), 1–26.
Swedberg, R. (2018). How to use Max Weber's ideal type in sociological analysis. *Journal of Classical Sociology, 18*(3), 181–196.
Szacki, J. (2011). *Tradycja: Przegląd problematyki [Tradition: An overview].* Warszawa: WUW.
Thum, G. (2011). *Uprooted: How Breslau became Wrocław during the century of expulsions.* Princeton, NJ: Princeton University Press.
Van Nieuwenhuyse, K. (2018). Torn between patriotic, civic and disciplinary aspirations. Evolving faces of Belgian and Flemish history education, from 1830 to the future. *Sprawy Narodowościowe. Seria Nowa, 50,* 1–16.
Van Nieuwenhuyse, K., & Wils, K. (2012). Remembrance education between history teaching and citizenship education. *Citizenship Teaching and Learning, 7*(2), 157–171.
Wertsch, J. V. (2002). *Voices of collective remembering.* Cambridge: Cambridge University Press.
Wertsch, J. V., & Roediger, H. L., III. (2008). Collective memory: Conceptual foundations and theoretical approaches. *Memory, 16*(3), 318–326.
Williams, G. A. (1982). *The welsh in their history.* London: Croom Helm.

Wimmer, A. (2008). The making and unmaking of ethnic boundaries: A multilevel process theory. *American Journal of Sociology, 113*, 970–1022.
Wojdon, J. (2017a). *Textbooks as propaganda: Poland under communist rule, 1944–1989*. London: Routledge.
Wojdon, J. (2017b). How to make school history more controversial? Controversies in history education in Poland. In H. Å. Elmersjö, A. Clark, & M. Vinterek (Eds.), *International perspectives on teaching rival histories: Pedagogical responses to contested narratives and the history wars* (pp. 157–179). London: Palgrave.
Wojdon, J. (2019). Poland. In L. Cajani, S. Lässig, & M. Repoussi (Eds.), *The Palgrave handbook of conflict and history education in the post-cold war era* (pp. 469–485). Cham: Palgrave.
Zaremba, M. (2001). *Nacjonalizm, komunizm, legitymizacja: Nacjonalistyczna legitymizacja władzy w komunistycznej Polsce [Nationalism, communism, legitimisation: Nationalist legitimisation of power in communist Poland]*. Warsaw: Trio.

3 Teaching history, celebrating nationalism

Introduction

In this chapter, we investigate how teachers themselves define the aims of history teaching in the context of different models of historical education. Firstly, we examine their views on why they teach history, demonstrating the significance of the nationalist model of education. Although the teachers whom we interviewed were not a homogeneous group, they generally saw historical education in terms of instilling national identity in pupils. Learning history is important for them because it enables students to acquire and strengthen their national identity and to develop an emotional bond with and loyalty to the Polish nation state. We also explore the apparent contradiction in teachers' statements. Teachers, on the one hand, believed that history is an objective science. On the other hand, they claimed that history should serve to strengthen the national identity. Paradoxically, the nationalist model of teaching history went hand in hand with naive epistemological realism. From a subjective–rational point of view, however, there is no contradiction here: the teachers ontologised the category of nation by situating it outside history as a permanent and self-evident element of reality. In their opinion, national history is not a politically and socially conditioned construction of reality but a reality per se. In this chapter, we also consider the few teachers who contested the nationalist model of history teaching in favour of the disciplinary approach. These few voices, which are in contrast to the views of other teachers, show even more clearly the specificity of the dominant nationalist model of history education.

Teaching history, teaching nationalism

Almost all the interviewed teachers looked at school education through the prism of nationalism. They emphasised the identitary functions of school history. Some teachers considered the nationalist aims of education to be so

DOI: 10.4324/9781003028529-3

obvious that they had trouble answering the question – we call such teachers conformists:

- What values do textbooks convey, and what do you think they should convey?
- Oh, Jesus! Such a difficult question. . . . I don't know what the textbook's authors thought. Maybe I should have probably read the introduction and memorised it . . . there's a lot of this patriotic element.

The teacher initially had difficulty in answering, but after a while she noted that the textbook places great emphasis on 'patriotism'. Later in the interview, she explained that attachment to the nation 'is very valuable and important and needs to be instilled in small children from the beginning'. She concluded that, during history lessons, we should 'awaken the awareness that we are Poles, that there's Poland here'.

Other teachers had no problem with answering and clearly underlined nationalist educational goals, regardless of the type of school at which they taught. One of the teachers said:

> respect for ancestors, for past . . . this is also an amazing lesson of patriotism; I think that every such lesson can pay homage to . . . demonstrate such love, heroism . . . that you can worship at least for a moment . . . arouse these emotions and reflections, this is, the patriotic attitude. . . . I set myself such goals.

Teachers spoke of love for the homeland, respect for ancestors, the need to make students aware of where they come from, what their roots and traditions are, the forming of national identity, respect for national symbols, and obligations to the Polish state. Their statements fit with the nationalist construction of reality, which assumes that nations are the basic element of reality and that national loyalty and duties towards the nation determine the identity of the individual.

Typically, teachers themselves did not use the term nationalism when talking about the aims of history education. Most often they said that they were patriots but not nationalists: 'I'm far away from nationalism, but on the other hand, I'm against marginalising national culture and customs, against absorbing everything from your surroundings and forgetting about our uniqueness'. Teachers even warned against nationalism but only identified it with extreme xenophobic attitudes. This practice of opposing 'healthy' patriotism to 'pathological' nationalism is quite common in Poland (Jaskulowski, 2003; Jaskulowski, Majewski, & Surmiak, 2018; Porter, 2000). In accordance with this common understanding, teachers associated their position with the positive term 'patriotism' and used the notion of nationalism only to refer to extreme ideologies or national attitudes, which they sometimes projected onto marginal extreme groups or national others, especially Ukrainians, Russians, and Germans. As Michael Billig (1995) noted, such a dichotomous contrast between nationalism and patriotism leads to naturalisation and banalisation of one's own nationalism. Our own nationalism, now called patriotism, ceases to be seen as a problem and is instead considered to be a matter of moral concern, as something that society lacks and something that can never be too much.

Although teachers agreed on the importance of nationalism (or 'patriotism', to use their terminology) in school history education, this does not mean that there were no differences between them. The conformists mainly stressed nationalist educational goals. A somewhat different approach was taken by the teachers whom we call moderate nationalists. The moderate nationalists shared the nationalist aims of school education but at the same time talked about other aims. They also indicated the need to develop more universal civic values and transnational as well as sub-national identities. They rarely spoke of global citizenship, however, and usually in this context they mentioned the European dimension, understood as the 'Europe of homelands'. For example, one of the teachers explained, 'I obviously believe that we should build a national identity and community, but without forgetting this regional level . . . without forgetting Europe, ... Let's build national pride . . . but with a sense of great caution and great responsibility'. The quotation demonstrates the conviction, typical of moderate nationalists, that history lessons should serve the development of national identity, but simultaneously they must also instil in pupils a regional and wider European identity, which brings this position closer to the civic model of teaching history. The moderate nationalists were also engaged in 'normative balancing' between communicating and imposing values (Wansik, Akkerman, Zuiker, & Wubbels, 2018). They emphasised the importance of the nation while leaving some freedom to the students. As one of the teachers said, 'I think that the role of a teacher should be, say, to emphasise some values but at the same time to leave students some freedom, some agency, because they are also intelligent persons'.

A more categorical position was taken by the teachers whom we call radical nationalists. For the radical nationalists, there was no room for negotiation: a nation is an unquestionable value. They defined the aims of historical education mainly in terms of imposing national identity on pupils. Moreover, radical nationalists believed that historical education does not currently perform its nationalising functions. They positioned themselves in opposition to the official educational policy, but de facto their approach fits into the nation-centred logic of the core curriculum and textbooks. They considered history to be one of the main school subjects and framed current education as being in crisis: there are not enough history lessons at school; moreover, history enjoys little prestige and is depreciated for being not very practical. As one of the teachers explained: 'It's taught that English or computer science are the most important (. . .) such things as our own identity, culture, . . . we forget about it; it's not so much forgetting, as deliberate action'. Such statements fit into the suspicion rhetoric typical of rightwing politicians (Jaskulowski, 2012). According to this rhetoric, behind the destruction of education stand the liberal and leftist elites, which, under pressure from international organisations, promote multiculturalism at the expense of Polish national identity. As another teacher said, 'today's world, well, we are moving away from this national approach; we are entering into such multiculturalism'.

According to the radical nationalists, the crisis in historical education also consisted of the fact that there is not enough content in textbooks to nationalise pupils. For example, one of the radical nationalists criticised the textbooks for various shortcomings, noting at the same time that he had enough freedom to correct these flaws on his own: 'I can modify, add something (. . .) to add cursed soldiers, 17th September, that is, the Soviet attack on Poland . . . Katyń. Such things that are not included or are only mentioned in textbooks'. This quotation demonstrates well what content the radical nationalists thought the textbooks lack. They paid particular attention to recent history and especially to the communist period. In their view, knowledge of communism is very important because it allows pupils to understand the origins of contemporary Polish politics and provides an opportunity to show them who was 'good' and who was 'bad' in recent Polish history, that is, who was on the side of Polish independence and who was its enemy. The radical nationalists had special esteem for the so-called cursed soldiers (members of the post-war anti-communist underground; Kończal, 2020), whom they perceived as a particularly valuable moral example for young people.

The radical nationalists also spoke in terms of the crisis about the pupils whom they saw as being indifferent to the nation. As one of the teachers puts it, 'it's difficult to shape these [patriotic] attitudes . . . among young people . . . because they're simply not interested in it'. They linked this alleged collapse of national feelings with the crisis of the so-called traditional family, which ceased to perform its pedagogical duties, and with the crisis of values in Polish society. They saw this crisis of values as being the result not only of various spontaneous processes, such as individualisation, consumerism, and de-traditionalisation, but also of deliberate action on the part of the liberal elite, which is dismantling patriotic education:

> It goes towards global history. . . . So what am I supposed to educate for? For globalization? So what generation will I educate? . . . [W]e

can talk about education to be European, but for me European culture is Greek philosophy, Roman law and Christianity, now it's upside down . . . the EU institutions relativise this and it's like jelly.

On a collective level, the lack of 'patriotism' was seen by the radical nationalists as a threat to the existence of the Polish nation because it weakens the national bonds. On an individual level, it makes pupils grow into amoral, selfish, and uprooted individuals. In line with the logic of nationalist ethics, the radical nationalists assumed that there is no morality without national belonging. One teacher explained, 'I constantly tell them [the pupils] that a man who does not know his own history is a worthless man'. The radical nationalists also assumed that national identity is something given that pupils simply have to discover or awaken: 'Well, we are Polish, our roots are here. Whether we want it or not, that is a fact'. Pupils can forget about their real identity, but, according to the radical nationalists, this will not change the fact that they are Poles; they will simply be 'bad' Poles, miserable people who live against their nature. The radical nationalists defined their role not only in didactical terms but also in moral terms: they saw themselves as the last real Poles whose mission is to nationalise the young generation to stop the erosion of patriotism that is threatening the existence of the Polish nation (Jaskulowski & Surmiak, 2017).

Between objectivity and ideology

Although the conformists, the radical nationalists, and the moderate nationalists differed in the importance that they attached to 'patriotism', they shared the belief that school history should play a nationalising function. Simultaneously, they expressed the conviction that history is an objective science. This belief seems to be quite widespread among Polish teachers: quantitative studies have shown that 98% of them define history in terms of objectivity (Burszta et al., 2019, p. 53). Teachers seem not to see a contradiction between the perception of history as a tool to strengthen identity and the perception of history as an objective science (which in itself is a questionable approach; Appleby, Hunt, & Jacob, 1994; Tucker, 2009; Wansink, Akkerman, Vermunt, Haenen, & Wubbels, 2017). As one teacher said:

> I think that history should be propagandist science . . . in the sense that history should build our self-esteem. Of course, without falsifying the past, we should represent the past in such a way as to instil pride among students. History should also be objective, but I appreciate more the value of developing a national identity and national pride.

On the one hand, teachers stated that it is necessary to tell the truth and be objective; on the other hand, they pointed out that history is a propaganda science that should inspire pride among students. Another teacher, a radical nationalist, noted:

> the teacher is supposed to convey the historical truth . . . but I cannot forget that . . . I have to de-mythologise. . . . For example, the People's Republic of Poland . . . everyone says 'it was a success, we ended the war, we rebuilt the country', and it turns out that we are still fighting and we have the cursed soldiers. And I have to turn it upside down so that they are not bandits but patriots.

On the one hand, the teacher spoke about historical truth; on the other hand, he suggested that he must show who was 'good' and who was 'bad' in history. The teacher glorified the cursed soldiers while presenting his teaching as debunking history in the name of historical truth. Paradoxically, it is a kind of propaganda of the People's Republic of Poland *à rebours*. While the communists presented the cursed soldiers as bandits, now the teacher sees them as patriotic heroes (Kończal, 2020). In the teacher's opinion, historical truth lies in an objective description of the facts and, at the same time, in assessing the past in unambiguous moral terms.

Statements combining a belief in objectivity with the conviction that history is a tool for strengthening national identity recurred in many interviews. How can this apparent inconsistency be explained? It seems that teachers are generally unable or unwilling to recognise the nationalist politics involved in representing the past in national terms (Jaskulowski & Surmiak, 2017). For teachers, national history is not so much an interpretation of the past that serves some political purpose but simply a reality per se and the past is inherently national: nations are real, distinct entities, a basic building block of social reality. According to teachers, nations are facts, not constructions conditioned by the dynamics of politics, discourse, and power. It seems that nationalism is so strongly internalised by teachers that they take it for granted. This lack of critical distance to national representations of the past is evident not only in open declarations but also in the habitual use of the pronouns 'we', 'us', and 'our' or the adverb 'here' (Billig, 1995). Teachers even talk in such categories about the distant past, including the early medieval Piast dynasty. They evoke the national 'we', which has a somewhat timeless quality. Such use of 'we' indicates suspension of time, which is typical of mythological thinking in which the present and the past exist simultaneously (Lowenthal, 1998). Teachers teach normative collective memory, which is both historical and ahistorical. It is historical in the sense that it refers to the past; however, it is ahistorical because it elevates 'the national' to the position of a timeless or eternal standard (Szacki, 2011). By suggesting that the Polish nation has existed since time immemorial, history is mythologised and transformed into nature and, in turn, nationalism is naturalised and depoliticised (Barthes, 1972).

This does not mean that all the teachers whom we interviewed perceived the nation entirely in ahistorical terms. Many teachers spoke about the evolution of the Polish nation's social base, noting that, in the Middle Ages, only the elite belonged to the nation. They considered that there was no qualitative difference between the medieval and the modern nation. It is still the same nation, the basic identity of which has not changed much over time. Teachers constituted the continuity of history in national terms: history is a predetermined unilinear process of becoming a nation, a process that moves in one direction towards the establishment of a modern Polish nation state. Even if the Polish nation in the Middle Ages consisted only of knight elites, it was predetermined that the national consciousness of lower social groups would be 'awakened' sooner or later. Teachers did not teach how national thinking came about, but they did teach thinking in national terms even if they criticised some simplified textbook content. For example, one of the teachers said:

> The Battle of Grunwald, which I was taught was a Polish victory . . . a Polish – German battle. However, the truth is completely different. First, it's not only a victory of the Poles . . . rather Lithuanians and Poles, and second, it's such an international battle, there wasn't a more international battle on Polish soil, because on the Teutonic Knights' side we have Englishmen and French, and on our side we actually have a whole mixture of Slavic groups.

On the one hand, the teacher criticised the simplified interpretations that portray the battle as a German–Polish clash. On the other hand, when talking about medieval knighthood, he used the contemporary categories 'Poles', 'Lithuanians', 'Englishmen', and 'French'. He spoke of knights serving under the command of Vladislaus IIagello as being on 'our side', inscribing the battle into a national narrative in which one and the same Polish nation is a collective subject. 'We' contemporary Poles differ little from old Polish medieval knights: their victories are ours. The teacher also slavicised Jagiełło's forces, overlooking for instance a contingent of Muslim Tatars, who speak Turkish, fighting on 'our side'.

Teachers interpellated pupils as members of the Polish community, which stretches not only in space but also in time, reaching back deep into the Middle Ages. According to the teachers, the aim of teaching history is to strengthen the national identity of students by rooting it in time, showing its persistence and constancy. The aim is not so much to teach the historian's workshop as to make students memorise the canonical history of Poland. As one of the teachers explained, 'I wrote all the dates on the board, we analysed what had happened in the different years. . . . [I]t turned out that one event depends on the other. Cause, effect, cause, effect'. One event brings with it another and they all form a linear cause-and-effect sequence, which leads from the medieval patrimony of Mieszko I to the contemporary Polish nation state. From the teachers' point of view, pupils need to know this canonical story, along with key figures and dates, because they form the foundation of their national identity and provide them with moral orientation in the world.

The preponderance of the nationalist model of historical education among teachers should not come as a surprise in the context of the already-discussed tradition of history teaching in Poland, which was routinely focused on promoting national identity. The influence of the dominant model of historiography at universities in Poland is also very important. This model is largely based on the 19th-century erudite concept of historiography developed by Leopold von Ranke. Although this model is obviously contested, it still enjoys considerable popularity in Poland (Jaskulowski, 2009; Jaskulowski et al., 2018; Topolski, 1996, 1998). The model assumes that history is an objective science aiming to describe the past *wie es eigentlich gewesen* [how things actually were]. According to the model, the key to the historical method is to establish new facts based on the analysis of primary sources. The facts are allegedly objective and independent of the theoretical and methodological context, any non-empirical assumptions must be rejected, historical inference is inductive, and historical knowledge is cumulative. The historian's task is to fill in the gaps in our knowledge of the past by discovering new facts until we finally have a complete picture of the past.

In this model, the historical method is reduced to the examination of critical sources and the establishing of new facts. Much less importance is attached to combining facts into a coherent narrative, conceptualising the subject of research, explaining social processes, or understanding human actions. Assuming that facts speak for themselves, it is enough simply to describe them without any prejudices or theoretical premises concerning, for example, the relationship between social structures and agency or rationality of human action (Dymkowski, 2003). Reluctance to theorise makes historians, when constructing their narratives, rely on common sense or ideology – usually nationalist in accordance with the traditional perception of history as the basis of national identity. Thus, on the one hand, historiography is understood as an objective and rigorous science due to its methods of examining primary sources. On the other hand, historians refer to nationalist categories that they consider to be natural and do not subject them to critical considerations (Jaskułowski et al., 2018; Kula, 2008, 2011).

During the communist era, for many historians, Marxist social theory served as a theoretical framework to structure their empirical research (Górny, 2007). However, after the democratic transition, most of the historians rejected it because it was associated with communist propaganda. The general crisis of meta-narration and the fragmentation of social theories further deepened historians' scepticism about social science. As a result, history in Poland remains largely an idiographic discipline. It is dominated by a simple chronological and detailed description reproducing commonsense beliefs and especially the nationalist construction of reality. This also translates into a way of educating history teachers at universities, who are socialised to this model of history. As Wojdon, who analysed academic textbooks for history didactics, wrote, 'the core of those books deals with the issues of school practice and concentrates on instilling "factual knowledge" and values – especially patriotism' (Wojdon, 2017, p. 171). The textbooks do not deal with teaching historical knowledge itself, and, if there are examples of analyses of historical sources, such examples are mainly used as an illustration of predetermined factual knowledge (Wojdon, 2017).

Contesting voices

Although the idiographic and nationalist model seems to dominate, it is not the only way of practising history in Poland. Discussions on the nature of historical knowledge have also emerged in Poland, influencing the views of historians, including history teachers (Domańska, Stobiecki, & Wiślicz, 2014). Among our interviewees, there were teachers who rejected the nationalist model of historiography – we call them the opponents. As we have already noted, some criticism of the dominant model was voiced by the moderate nationalists. However, the moderate nationalists only questioned certain aspects of the hegemonic concept, such as projecting the existence of fully fledged nations into the distant past, and they did not question its very logic. They were critical of the dominant narrative, indicating its limitation, but they did not apply the same criteria to their own narration. They simply wanted to replace one narrative with another, better, true one. They aimed to develop critical historical awareness among pupils but not genetic awareness sensitive to the limitations, contextuality, and contingency of any historical knowledge, including our own (Rüssen, 2004).

The opponents went further in their criticism and challenged the three most important points of the dominant model of historical education, which, in their opinion, were closely linked, namely the treatment of history as an instrument of nationalisation, the concentration of teaching on content instead of on the foundations of the discipline, and the naive realist epistemology. For example, one of the opponents argued that the core curriculum and textbooks treat a nation:

> [A]s if it's really some kind of really existing entity, and not some construct that emerges at a certain point in time . . . the whole large historiographic debate about what a nation actually is, when it arises, why . . . it doesn't actually appear in history textbooks.

In the opinion of the opponents, the lack of problematisation of a nation is due not only to the fact that the textbooks did not take into account the contemporary academic debate on the constructed and contingent nature of nations but also to a manifestation of a wider problem. It results from the neglect of a disciplinary approach to history and the lack of reflection on the perspectivity and political entanglement of history. Let us quote a little more from an opponent, because it illustrates very well the opponents' way of thinking, which sharply contrasts with the prevailing approach among teachers:

> This is a broader problem . . . history would be a fantastic tool to demonstrate how much of what exists now is contingent, temporary, and changeable, but it's actually used to show exactly the opposite . . . to naturalise what exists now. . . . The spirit of the misread Hegel hovers over it, the core curriculum tells us that all had a goal, and we are that goal . . . the nation . . . and that is disastrous . . . history really should be the discipline about revolution, it should teach that the world is changing unbelievably in such an uncontrolled and unpredictable way, that history has no purpose, history has no direction, and we don't know this past at all, we either discover it or reconstruct it non-stop; there is a methodological dispute here, whether we discover the past or create it, but we constantly reinterpret it, we use the knowledge of the past for political purposes, this is not said at school either, because school history relies on the 19th-century myth of the historian as an uninvolved person. . . . This is not true. The historian is involved in various disputes extremely strongly, and history is . . . a politicised discipline.

As the earlier quote demonstrates, the opponents criticised not only the treatment of nations as real and fixed groups and the presentation of their history in teleological terms but, above all, also the lack of discussion on the nature of the historical process and the neglect of the disciplinary approach. In their opinion, school history is based on an anachronistic view of history as static and closed knowledge. As one teacher puts it, 'the drawback of all textbooks is that ... they give the false impression that history is ... some package of closed knowledge. ... History as a discipline doesn't appear in the school at all'. They criticised the textbooks for focusing on content-related knowledge and overlooking history as a studying process that is socially, politically, and culturally positioned. Instead, school history refers to coherent and ready-made knowledge about a nation, which pupils must memorise. It does not take into account the concept of contingency and lack of determination but rather presupposes in advance that it is obvious and indisputable that history is a unidirectional process in which nations gradually develop and that a national perspective is not one of the possible ways of interpreting the past but a natural or God-given order of things. The opponents criticised the reification of nations and naive epistemological realism, which they rejected as being incompatible with the contemporary methodology and theory of history.

Having criticised the lack of a disciplinary approach to history at school and the domination of nationalism, the opponents noted not only the negative educational consequences (schools do not teach history as a discipline) but also the harmful political consequences:

> I blame the schools for this turn to nationalism. I don't think that it comes from nowhere and it's really not the case that boys, because they are mainly boys, who riot during the 11th of November [the Polish Independence Day] are mostly socially excluded. . . . [T]here are a lot of law students and history students . . . this message of school history has a strong influence on those who are interested in history.

In the opinion of the opponents, the way in which history is taught leads to the production and strengthening of negative attitudes and behaviours among pupils towards people regarded as 'others'.

Conclusions

In this chapter, we analysed the way in which teachers defined the aims of school history education. We showed that they predominantly defined the objectives of education in nationalist terms. Teachers generally reproduced the hegemonic concept of nation-centred history teaching aimed at forming bonds with the nation among students. They did, however, differ in some respects. We distinguished four types of teachers. The conformists accepted the core curriculum and the textbooks without much deliberation. The radical nationalists believed that the core curriculum and textbooks were not nationalist enough and stressed the need to strengthen the national message.

The moderate nationalists did not deny the national educational goals but at the same time stressed the need to develop more universal and local identities, which brought them closer to the civic model. These categories of teachers were united by the belief that history is an objective science and, at the same time, an instrument for nationalising pupils. We explained this combination of naive epistemological realism and ideological commitment of teachers by indicating their tacit acceptance of the nationalist construction of reality, which they treated as reality per se. They overlooked the role of nationalist politics in their understanding of the goals of history teaching because they considered the nationalist construction of reality to be self-evident and natural. A small group of opponents rejected the nationalist model. The opponents not only criticised the focus of school education on the nation but also questioned the naive realist epistemology. They emphasised the active role of the historian in historical cognition and the need to teach the basics of history as a discipline, which placed them within the disciplinary model of teaching history.

References

Appleby, J., Hunt, L., & Jacob, M. (1994). *Telling the truth about history*. New York: Norton.
Barthes, R. (1972). *Mythologies*. New York: Hill and Wang.
Billig, M. (1995). *Banal nationalism*. London: Sage Publishing House.
Burszta, W. J., Dobrosielski, P., Jaskulowski, K., Majbroda, K., Majewski, P., & Rauszer, M. (2019). *Naród w szkole: Historia i nacjonalizm w polskiej edukacji szkolnej [The nation at school: History and nationalism in Polish school education]*. Gdańsk: Katedra.
Domańska, E., Stobiecki, R., & Wiślicz, T. (Eds.). (2014). *Historia – dziś. Teoretyczne problemy wiedzy o przeszłości [History – today. Theoretical problems of knowledge about the past]*. Kraków: Universitas.
Dymkowski, M. (2003). *Wprowadzenie do psychologii historycznej [Introduction to historical psychology]*. Gdańsk: GWP.
Górny, M. (2007). *Przede wszystkim ma być naród. Marksistowskie historiografie w Europie Środkowo-Wschodniej [First of all there must be a nation. Marxist historiographies in Central Eastern Europe]*. Warszawa: Trio.
Jaskulowski, K. (2003). *Mityczne przestrzenie nacjonalizmu [Mythical dimensions of nationalism]*. Torun: Adam Marszalek.
Jaskulowski, K. (2009). *Nacjonalizm bez narodów: Nacjonalizm w koncepcjach anglosaskich nauk społecznych [Nationalism without nations: Nationalism in anglophone social sciences]*. Wroclaw: Monografie FNP.
Jaskulowski, K. (2012). *Wspólnota symboliczna [Symbolic community]*. Gdansk: Katedra.
Jaskułowski, K., Majewski, P., & Surmiak, A. (2018). Teaching the nation: History and nationalism in Polish school history education. *British Journal of Sociology of Education, 39*(1), 77–91.

Jaskulowski, K., & Surmiak, A. (2017). Teaching history, teaching nationalism: A qualitative study of history teachers in a Polish post-industrial town. *Critical Studies in Education, 58*(1), 36–51.

Kończal, K. (2020). The invention of the 'cursed soldiers' and its opponents: Postwar partisan struggle in contemporary Poland. *East European Politics and Societies, 34*(1), 67–95.

Kula, M. (2008). *O co chodzi w historii? [What is history about?]*. Warszawa: WUW.

Kula, M. (2011). *Naród, historia i... dużo kłopotów [Nation, historia and... many troubles]*. Kraków: Universitas.

Lowenthal, D. (1998). *The heritage crusade and the spoils of history*. Cambridge: Cambridge University Press.

Porter, B. (2000). *When nationalism began to hate: Imagining modern politics in nineteenth century Poland*. Oxford: Oxford University Press.

Rüssen, J. (2004). Historical consciousness: Narrative structure, moral function and ontogenetic development. In P. Seixas (Ed.), *Theorizing historical consciousness* (pp. 63–85). Toronto: Toronto University Press.

Szacki, J. (2011). *Tradycja: Przegląd problematyki [Tradition: An overview]*. Warszawa: WUW.

Topolski, J. (1996). *Jak się piszę i rozumie historię [How history is written and understood]*. Warsaw: Rytm.

Topolski, J. (1998). *Od Achillesa do Beatrice de Planisolles: Zarys historii historiografii [From Achilles to Beatrice de Planisolles. An outline of the history of historiography]*. Warsaw: Rytm.

Tucker, A. (Ed.). (2009). *A companion to philosophy of history and historiography*. Oxford: Oxford University Press.

Wansik, B., Akkerman, S., Zuiker, I., & Wubbels, T. (2018). Where does teaching multiperspectivity in history education begin and end? An analysis of the uses of temporality. *Theory & Research in Social Education, 48*(4), 495–527.

Wansink, B. G., Akkerman, S. F., Vermunt, J. D., Haenen, J. P., & Wubbels, T. (2017). Epistemological tensions in prospective Dutch history teachers' beliefs about the objectives of secondary education. *Journal of Social Studies Research, 41*(1), 11–24.

Wojdon, J. (2017). How to make school history more controversial? Controversies in history education in Poland. In H. Å. Elmersjö, A. Clark, & M. Vinterek (Eds.), *International perspectives on teaching rival histories: Pedagogical responses to contested narratives and the history wars* (pp. 157–179). London: Palgrave.

4 Nationalism, but what kind?

Introduction

In this chapter, we explore the different types of nationalism represented by teachers. Our analysis focuses on the conformists, moderate nationalists, and radical nationalists; we pay less attention to the opponents because they did not consider that history should be used to promote nationalism. We discuss the differences between teachers, concentrating on the four issues that divided them the most. Firstly, we investigate how teachers understood the Polish nation, that is, whether they defined it in an inclusive or an exclusive way. Then, we explore the extent to which the teachers focused on the history of the Polish nation in contrast to general history. We then consider how teachers imagined obligations towards the nation. The main difference between the teachers was that some of them were in favour of educating pupils in readiness to sacrifice themselves for the nation, including giving their lives. Others criticised this approach and advocated the development of civic virtues among pupils: solid fulfilment of their daily duties and public engagement. The last difference concerns the glorifying versus critical approach to Polish history: some teachers believed that it is necessary to teach mainly about the positive aspects of national history to incite national pride among pupils, while others, in turn, felt that the dark sides of national history should also be discussed.

Civic and ethnic nationalism?

The classic typology assumes that nationalism takes two basic forms: ethnic and civic (Jaskulowski, 2003, 2010; Kohn, 1944). Ethnic nationalism defines a nation as a cultural community or in terms of common descent, while civic nationalism views a nation as a political community. The dichotomy has been criticised many times, but, after some modifications, it may still be useful as it draws attention to an important point, namely that

DOI: 10.4324/9781003028529-4

forms of nationalism differ in their degree of inclusion (Jaskulowski, 2010; Kuzio, 2002; Kymlicka, 2001). Modifying the dichotomy, we distinguish three types of nationalism. Firstly, ethnic exclusionary nationalism refers to a common origin or, in extreme cases, to phenotypic criteria of national belonging, such as skin colour. Secondly, cultural nationalism emphasises the importance of cultural factors as national membership criteria, but culture is understood here in an essentialist and thick way, which makes this nationalism relatively closed, although it does not exclude completely new potential members but makes assimilationist requirements that only a few are able and willing to meet. Thirdly, civic nationalism refers to political criteria and public culture: new members need to acquire only the minimum elements of a titular nation's culture to participate in public life (e.g. learn the official language) (Jaskulowski, 2019; Kymlicka, 2001).

Our quantitative survey suggested that ethnic nationalism was the dominant type of nationalism among the teachers: 74% of them considered blood ties to be important for national belonging, and 14% viewed these ties as being of moderate importance (Burszta et al., 2019). In the opinion of teachers, the blood criterion is a necessary but not sufficient condition of nationality because the respondents who indicated the blood factor also pointed to other criteria. In total, 92% of the teachers considered blood ties to be an important or moderately important factor connecting a nation, which would mean that they are in favour of an extremely exclusionary concept of the Polish nation. Interestingly, the interviewed teachers did not mention blood at all, which can be explained in two ways. Firstly, during the interviews, the teachers did not have a predetermined list of nationality criteria (as in quantitative research): they did not have any suggestion that blood matters and did not have to respond to this idea. Secondly, during the interviews, the teachers could avoid statements that might put them in a bad light, for instance, by suggesting that they are racists.

Although the teachers did not speak explicitly about the blood criterion, this does not mean that they do not support the closed concept of a nation. It was mainly radical nationalists who referred to such a concept, as shown by them defining a nation in organic terms: 'everyone must be aware that a tree that doesn't care about its roots will die. Similarly, if they aren't aware of their roots . . . well, without roots there is no future. Speaking diplomatically'. The teacher stressed that her statement was diplomatic and that she had toned down her message and had not spoken fully openly. It can be assumed that if she had spoken openly, she would have emphasised more strongly the organic and natural character of the nation. Naturalist language suggested that teachers equate biological with cultural reproduction. The radical nationalists also referred to cultural nationalism by relying on a thick understanding of national culture. In their opinion, the Polish nation was united by a homogeneous culture, a common language, and a common history, the essence of which was the 1000-year-old relationship between the Polish nation and 'Christianity' as they metonymically spoke about Catholicism. As one of the teachers explained: 'we have Catholic civilisation . . . everything comes from Christianity, and that is what is presented'. It should be added that some conformists and moderate nationalists also referred to the 'thick' cultural understanding of the Polish nation. However, it was the radical nationalists who most clearly emphasised that the Polish nation is a Catholic community of destiny, 'rooted' deeply in history, with a relatively unchanging identity. The radical nationalists tended to define the nation in a way that reflected the traditional right-wing collectivist understanding of Polishness as belonging to a religiously and culturally homogeneous white community (Porter, 2000). At the other extreme, there were teachers who referred to the concept of a nation typical of civil nationalism – mainly moderate nationalists and sometimes conformists. For example, one of the teachers, when explaining what kind of attitudes he taught, evoked the pre-war concept of statehood, which stood in opposition to the ethnic nationalist conception of the state:

> [D]emocracy, civic attitude, because they're very negative towards democracy. . ., this is something that before the war was called statehood. . . . I mean to instil some general and fundamental principles in them, that the state is ours, that they've to respect it, that . . . they've to respect and enforce certain democratic principles.

In the teacher's interpretation, the pre-war tradition of statehood is democratic and open. This is a certain paradox, because the symbol of this tradition is Józef Piłsudski, who introduced dictatorial rule in Poland in 1926. This is a symptom of a broader tendency in Polish historical discourse to glorify Piłsudski and the Second Republic of Poland and to ignore its heritage of authoritarianism and social and political exclusion (Hein-Kircher, 2008).

The moderate nationalists defined the Polish nation in terms of a common culture but stressed its diversity and openness. As one of the moderate nationalists said, 'Such attitudes should be formed . . . open-mindedness, with all due respect for national heroes, national symbols, colours . . . but also with respect, well, for minorities'. As another teacher briefly puts it, 'history . . . shows that it doesn't matter what your ethnic origin is. . . . We all live in Poland'. Although the moderate nationalists left some room for national minorities, the openness of some of them was limited. For example, one of the teachers explained that, when she talks about minorities, she always tries to show her pupils 'that the other . . . isn't always the enemy. . . . I try to demonstrate by historical examples that such communities can bring much good for society'. Thus, she talks about minorities in terms of objectified otherness; minorities are seen as outsiders who exist for the benefit of the dominant group (Bryan, 2009; Jaskulowski, Majewski, & Surmiak, 2018).

Poland-first nationalism versus international Poland

The teachers also differed in their view of how much emphasis should be placed on the history of Poland in comparison with general history. The radical nationalists believed that there were few themes devoted to Polish history in the core curriculum and too much general history (which they identified with the history of Western Europe and North America). Some radical nationalists even postulated the separation of Polish from general history and suggested teaching it as a separate subject called patriotic education. They followed the proposal of Roman Giertych, the leader of the radical nationalist party of the League of Polish Families, who was Deputy Prime Minister and Minister of Education between 2006 and 2007. As one of the teachers said, 'I like very much the desiderata of the unpopular Minister of Education Roman Giertych, who proposes setting up separate classes on Polish history' (Jaskulowski et al., 2018; Shibata, 2013).

The radical nationalists accused the liberal elites who ruled Poland after 1989, in their opinion, of putting too much emphasis on general history in education. According to them, liberal elites suffer from an inferiority complex towards the West, which they try to imitate – hence, the emphasis on Western history in textbooks. Liberal elites have allowed an asymmetric situation to arise: Polish pupils have to learn Western history, while in Western schools Polish history is ignored. For radical nationalists, this is a manifestation of a lack of national dignity. Here, we can again hear echoes of the 'politics on the knees' metaphor used by various right-wing politicians to criticise the liberals for being too service-minded towards Western countries (Jaskulowski, 2019). For example, one of the teachers explained which history students should learn at school:

> Above all, the history of their own country. I just don't give a shit about America or something, but they [students] must know the history of Poland. . . . For me, there are too many other nations. We're probably the only country where we teach so many histories of other nations.

Although the radical nationalists agreed on the primary importance of Polish history, they differed in their perception of the uniqueness of Poland.

Some of them believed that Poland has an exceptional history compared with other countries. For example, one of the teachers compared Polish and the US history:

> We've ... a really rich history. I think that a few countries have such a history. ... I always laugh, because they [students] say to me that in America pupils study the constitution, and I say, it's because they don't have too much history. ... [I]t [American history] starts at the end of eighteenth century, so what they can do in history classes ... they study the constitution.

They mentioned three aspects of the uniqueness of Polish history. They noted that the Polish nation has developed a particularly rich national culture based on Christian values. They also stressed that Poles demonstrated exceptional heroism in the past and always fought passionately for independence. They also spoke of the enormous extent of the suffering experienced by the Polish nation, which was repeatedly invaded by its neighbours, particularly Germany and Russia. This was also sometimes associated with their anger at allied countries, such as the United Kingdom, France, and the US, which they accused of abandoning or betraying Poland, for example, at Yalta in 1945. According to the radical nationalists, those countries that invaded or betrayed Poland in the past have often developed economically and have a dominant position in international politics today, although they do not have the moral right to it. As one of the teachers puts it, 'those states which thrive today, they betrayed us many times' (Jaskulowski & Majewski, 2020). In accordance with the romantic paradigm of Polish nationalism, some radical nationalists also believed that past suffering enriches Poland morally and that Poland has a moral mission to restore international politics, especially European politics (Walicki, 1994; Zubrzycki, 2006). Again, it echoes the rhetoric of some PiS politicians, who suggested that Poland should have more say in European politics to compensate for the historical injustice inflicted on her in the past.

Some radical nationalists criticised martyrdom, believing, in accordance with the Endecja tradition, that there is no point in giving suffering any special status (Porter, 2000). For example, one radical nationalist criticised the focus on defeats:

> The entire theme is devoted to ... the November and January Uprisings. Especially the latter, it was an unprecedented defeat ... and there is too much, ... the Warsaw Uprising ... of course all the glory to the participants for their heroism, it is undeniable, but it was a failure.

This group of radical nationalists emphasised that history is, by its very nature, a domain of rivalry and struggle between nations, in which there are no moral principles but tough national interests (Porter, 2000). Therefore, pupils should not be persuaded that suffering gives Poland a special moral right but should be taught through history lessons how to take care of Polish national interests.

> [O]ur Polish point of view . . . Polish national interest. . . . Each nation . . . teaches history from its own perspective . . . we from the Polish, the Chinese from the Chinese, right, and that's good. . . . [T]his is how it should be because this is our point of view . . . we have to teach Polish history.

The other teachers, in contrast to the radical nationalists, believed that Polish history dominates the core curriculum and textbooks but evaluated it differently. The conformists generally believed that this focus on Polish history in Polish schools was understandable and obvious. They argued that one cannot teach everything as the content would be too extensive, so a selection must be made. It is natural – they claimed – that the most important thing for Polish pupils should be Polish history. In any case, they added that the students are indeed primarily interested in the history of Poland, which is closest to them and to which they are and should be emotionally connected.

The moderate nationalists, similar to the conformists, defined the history curriculum as focusing mainly on Polish history. However, unlike the conformists, they saw nothing self-evident in this and wondered whether the curriculum focused too much on Poland: 'I don't have a clear opinion whether there should be such overwhelming information on the history of Poland. I know we're Poles, blah blah . . . sincerely speaking, there is too much, this content is so extensive and detailed'. The moderate nationalists raised two points. Firstly, as we have already noted, the moderate nationalists aimed to teach history to strengthen the national identity of pupils but in the broader context of more universal identities. It is, therefore, not surprising that they criticised the excessive focus on Polish history and wanted it to be seen in a broader international context. The moderate nationalists, much more strongly than the conformists, underlined that Polish history is linked to the history of other countries. Some stressed the importance of ties with Western countries, others those with Europe, and some, like teachers from Upper Silesia, highlighted the links with Germany. In the opinion of the latter, the textbooks say very little about the influence of German culture on Polish culture because this does not fit into the concept of dominant Polishness, which is defined in opposition to Germany (Jaskulowski & Majewski, 2020). They believed that, for political reasons, history is presented in a distorted way in textbooks: 'I can't wait for the common Polish – German textbook. As far as I know, they are working on it . . . maybe at last history will be written by historians, not by politicians'. Some moderate nationalists even resembled their opponents in arguing that overfocusing on Polish history combined with the conviction that Polish history is unique is dangerous because it can produce xenophobes.

Secondly, the moderate nationalists criticised the focus on Polish history for methodological reasons, so to speak. They argued that focusing on Poland makes it difficult to explain the 'logic' of the historical process to students. They noted that the history of other nations is presented in a sketchy way and the events in question are taken out of context and not set on a chronological axis. This makes it difficult for pupils to understand many processes and events. They stressed that the history of other societies is discussed only as a background that allows students to grasp the specificity of Poland better: 'they only appear at such moments in order to understand the history of Poland, i.e. after contact with the history of Poland or to show that Poland takes something from those civilisations'.

However, the moderate nationalists were not a homogeneous group, and there were teachers among them who believed that more time should be devoted to the history of other nations, precisely because, without this knowledge, students will not be able to understand what happened in Poland. Despite the emphasis on general history, the attitude of these moderate nationalists is in line with the Polonocentric logic of historical education. According to this perspective, universal history should be taught primarily as a background for Polish history: 'We could present a general history, but in the sense that this history is a background for the history of Poland'. Some moderate nationalists even resembled radical nationalists but showed greater attachment to constructivist teaching methods than the latter. For example, one of the teachers said:

> There's such an overload with . . . detailed content, and there's a lack of such an analysis of . . . causes and effects . . . such historical thinking needs to be developed in some way, using some examples . . . reading primary sources and then making your own opinions. . . . I'd be inclined to confine some content, especially general history content, such as the history of America, Asia, and the Far East. Let's say that, even at the student level, if we ask a student from the US what they know about Europe. . ., it [their knowledge] is miserable . . . but in our country it is required at a more than extensive level.

The teacher criticised the fact overload because it does not leave space for more engaging teaching. He proposed revising the core curriculum by limiting topics on common history, which for him is less important than Polish history. In addition, he raised the argument, characteristic of the radical nationalists, that students in Western countries learn mainly their national history and that this should not be different in Poland.

Celebratory nationalism versus critical nationalism

Another difference between teachers concerns how to teach Polish history. Two opposing discourses can be distinguished: the glorious approach to history and more critical ones, which to varying degrees were visible in the interviews. Although it is difficult to assign one type of discourse to one category of teachers, the glorious approach to history was the most typical of radical nationalists and to some extent of conformists. The radical nationalists believed that they should focus primarily on glorious events and avoid discussing controversial topics. As one of them explained, 'If we're to continue to develop this nation, to be a nation, to be distinct.... We've to show some glorious events, right, from the past in order to build, I don't know, national pride'. That is why the radical nationalists criticised the core curriculum and textbooks for placing too little emphasis on building national pride:

> Having read these textbooks, I've the impression that they're too passive... there were just some battles. There is no such pathos connected with the fact that we, the Poles won, right. It could be done... with more enthusiasm, so that the enthusiasm could capture the students; this is my role here... I always try to emphasise it, so that... children wouldn't feel that we're an inferior or weaker nation. Because history shows many such glorious moments of which we should be proud.

The radical nationalists reported that they build pride among their pupils by referring mainly to political and military history because, in their opinion, this type of history makes it possible to show the greatness of Poland. For example, one of the teachers reported that the students asked her in class what she thought of Putin's alleged suggestions to divide Ukraine between Poland and Russia. She replied that they should look at the map and asked themselves to which country Ukraine belonged. Then the pupils shouted: 'This belonged to us!', and she said, 'You see, Putin was right.... He also looked through textbooks'. Although she clarified that she was kidding to a certain extent, at the same time, she explained to the students that Putin's proposal fits the logic of Polish history (Jaskulowski & Majewski, 2020). This passage is also interesting because it suggests that radicals see relationships between peoples as a kind of Hobbesian state of nature. As the quoted teacher argued, 'we must show . . . that this world of big politics is brutal. Every state minds only its own interests'. Defining international relations in terms of the battlefield was characteristic of the integral nationalism represented in Poland by ND, whose traditions to some extent are continued today by PiS (Alter, 1994; Cadier & Szulecki, 2020; Porter, 2000). The radical nationalists spoke of a brutal struggle for their interests but at the same time claimed that Poland was much less egoistic than other states and, unlike its allies, always kept its obligations: 'If we signed treaties . . . we took our commitments seriously'. Moreover, they stressed that, although Poland has been in a difficult situation many times, it has rarely compromised its integrity: 'we the Polish haven't calculated too often; we tried our best to get out of trouble with honour'. The radical nationalists stressed that too little emphasis is placed in textbooks on this national honour: 'I just try to communicate this to children, that this honour is the most important. Because a man with honour won't become a thief, a thug, a corrupt man. . . . You don't find this in textbooks, that we the Polish have such a national honour'. The radical nationalists took to extremes the nationalist assumption that, without attachment to a nation, there is no individual morality. National honour means that a real Pole will never be a bad person (Jaskulowski & Majewski, 2020).

National honour also means that Poles have never been aggressors but have always just defended themselves. In this context, the radical nationalists stressed that Poles do not have to apologise to anyone for their history: 'that we're inferior . . . that we've to apologise, to be ashamed, this is absolutely unacceptable, and they [students] also feel this way. . . . So I think that we should strongly stuff pupils' heads with such conviction'. Such an approach again reflects the right-wing PiS ideology with its criticism of the so-called shame pedagogy and the metaphor of Poland rising from its knees. Right-wing politicians have criticised those historians who focus on the harm inflicted by Poles in the past and condemned politicians who publicly apologise for historical offences. They have argued that state-sponsored history should be used to increase the self-confidence and pride of Poles, which is a condition for increasing Poland's international status. The radical nationalists are concerned about Poland's international position and teach history in such a way that students are proud of Poland's significance and strength. They do not give students many opportunities to question this approach to history. Although the radical nationalists declare the value of the discussion, they set clear boundaries. Firstly, they see history in dichotomic terms, which requires unequivocal assessments: 'we need to say explicitly that evil is evil, treachery is treachery'. Secondly, while critically discussing Polish history, the students, according to the radicals, 'have to appreciate the sacrifices of those who gave their lives for their fatherland' (Cadier & Szulecki, 2020; Jaskulowski & Majewski, 2020).

The radical nationalists attached a great deal of importance to making pupils proud by celebrating national heroes, especially political and military figures, such as the aforementioned so-called cursed soldiers (Hutchins, 2011; Kończal, 2020). As one of the radical nationalists explained:

> [T]his is the best way to teach young people ... by using the examples of national heroes who fought not only in Poland but also abroad. By bringing the lives of these people closer to the pupils, they're somehow learning such attitudes.

In their opinion, the heroes with which the students could identify themselves are not sufficiently presented in school education: 'Unfortunately, the textbooks lack heroes, such as strong characters, authorities'. Showing the example of the heroes, it is possible not only to incite national pride among pupils but also to demonstrate clearly the aforementioned unequivocal moral judgements, which the textbooks also lack: 'I mean, the distinction between good and evil isn't quite so clear, I'd say that everything is so blurred in it'.

It should be added, however, that some radical nationalists wanted to evoke pride not only by celebrating political and military characters but also by evoking cultural or economic history:

> The golden age [16th century] is far too little presented; it should be divided into a multitude of themes, demonstrating the strength, power, significance, but also the level of development, that we're equal to Europe ... then we'd have nothing to be ashamed of. We're at the level of France or England, we're ahead of Spain or Germany, so it should be more strongly emphasised, but it's not now.

They put particular emphasis on showing that there were times in history that Poland was the cultural and economic centre of Europe, aiming to arouse pupils' admiration for their ancestors' achievements and instil national pride among them. However, as we noted, their main focus was on military and political history, especially modern history.

At the other end of the spectrum, there were teachers who expressed concerns about this type of history teaching. Such voices can be found among both the conformists and the moderate nationalists. One of the teachers, for example, noted that it is good that history arouses pride, but he wonders whether it sometimes goes too far:

> that's a problem . . . history evokes emotions and without those emotions . . . it's basically so dull and bland; if someone is interested in this history, it's because somewhere there are these emotions. And unfortunately . . . if we talk about the wars which the Republic of Poland waged in the 17th century, it's treated a bit like a football match. We won well, we gave the Russians a shot. . ., I don't know if it's good or bad . . . it arouses pride in them [pupils] . . . a kind of pride in the fact that this Republic was once so strong and great.

It is characteristic that even the moderate nationalists spoke about past battles in terms of 'we'. Nor were they completely opposed to arousing national pride among the pupils, but they feared emphasising it too much, as this could lead to xenophobia and prejudice:

> And after the lessons about the war [the pupils say]: 'how good is that we don't learn German, I'll never learn German' . . . . I tell them to distinguish between the past and the present, why should your German colleague be guilty of this, or the German language? Prejudices and stereotypes, that's what our people feed on, really.

The moderate nationalists also believed that national pride should be aroused by referring primarily to cultural, scientific, or economic achievements, unlike the radical nationalists. The moderate nationalists also emphasised more strongly the need to look critically at the history of Poland and to discuss events that do not put Poles in a good light: 'for me there are too few negative things. . . . I understand that national history and identity is created by summing up positive events. . ., but some part . . . should be devoted to various political mistakes'. For example, moderate nationalism takes a critical stance towards the cursed soldiers, who, for the radical nationalists, were unquestionable heroes in accordance with official memory politics (Kończal, 2020). As one of the moderate nationalists explained:

> There's an order to organise. . . . The National Day of the Cursed Soldiers at school, when I talk to the 6th grade. . . [I]t's not only glory for those who fought, when the communists came here . . . but we also show figures that are not very glorious. Well, in my grandmother's memoirs, they were bandits, not partisans. . . . [T]hey murdered a peasant because he took land, or a policeman. . . . Well, there is no such content in the textbook.

Nationalism, but what kind? 53

The moderate nationalists did not shy away from presenting the 'dark' sides of national history, justifying this with pragmatic reasons: we need to know 'our' wrongdoings to avoid making similar mistakes in the future. However, some moderate nationalists also spoke of the need to develop critical historical awareness among pupils and saw their role as undermining simplified historical narratives (Rüssen, 2004). For example, one moderate nationalist explained that it provokes pupils to look critically at auto-stereotypes:

> I like it very much . . . when we start talking about Polish hurrah-patriotism and great achievements; I ask them why we have so few Nobel Prize winners . . . we discuss, right, about Poles and how wonderful these Poles are, I recall the title of such an Italian film. . . . 'Ugly, Dirty and Bad'. I ask why Poland has the lowest consumption of soap in the European Union, I ask why we have very pejorative expressions about all other nations . . . and, at the same time, when they say about us, stupid Poles, we feel offended.

The moderate nationalists practised critical history; that is, they taught pupils to challenge the stereotypical and simplified approaches to Polish history. However, they did not apply the same critical tools to their own narrative, which they presented as true. They developed a critical historical consciousness among students but not a genetic one (Rüssen, 2004). Moreover, even moderate nationalists warned that historical lessons should not be too critical and that certain limits should be set in discussions on controversial issues: 'It should be kept under control so that we don't fall into such historical relativism that there are events that can be interpreted in very different ways'.

The conformists' approach to controversial issues was somewhat different, and they stressed that they were unlikely to discuss such issues. The conformists mainly pointed out the lack of time and the need to focus on preparing students for tests:

> [C]ontroversial subjects aren't taken into account at all. . . . Not because they're difficult, forbidden subjects, but because it takes a lot of time to pursue such controversial subjects. Unfortunately, there isn't much time . . . now everything is done to prepare for the exam. . . . In the past, you could do more enjoyable things, there was more time for that.

Other teachers also talked about the lack of time and the pressure to prepare pupils for the tests, a kind of audit culture that imposes various restrictions, for example, related to the need to demonstrate 'measurable' learning outcomes (Power, 1997; Shore & Wright, 2015). However, the conformists stressed this most strongly and used it to justify their avoidance of difficult subjects. They accepted the basics and school textbooks quite passively, reproducing an uncritical form of nationalism focused primarily on the achievements and heroic deeds of the Polish nation.

Militarist nationalism versus mundane nationalism

The teachers in all categories, apart from the opponents, agreed that they had to develop loyalty to the nation. However, they understood the nature of this loyalty differently. There were two main patterns of loyalty, which we call militarist nationalism and mundane nationalism (Jaskulowski et al., 2018). The radical nationalists had the strongest views and generally stressed that loyalty to a nation is about willingness to fight for it and readiness to sacrifice your life for it. As one of the teachers explained, 'patriotism – as far as history is concerned, there's a lot of emphasis on it. First of all, there's the Second World War, so it's a heroism associated with the fight against the occupant'. Another radical nationalist described how he discussed the annexation of Crimea by Russia and the war in Donbas with pupils in an LSS. He reported that he was surprised that the pupils began to wonder where they would escape to from the war if Russia invaded Poland. He was worried that teenagers did not show any readiness to die for their homeland: 'as for the recent events in Ukraine, the dominant theme was where to flee, rather than what to do to defend the homeland, which was quite sad'. For the teacher, the ideal of patriotism relies on eagerness to fight for the nation. This kind of loyalty to the nation is symbolically represented in epic stories about wars and uprisings and exemplified by the figure of a male knight, insurgent, or soldier who is ready to give his life for his homeland. The radical nationalists viewed the past as a collection of heroic deeds – role models to be internalised by pupils. They paid special attention to the cursed soldiers, whom they saw as a telling and vivid example of heroes from quite a recent history, which could speak to the imagination of their pupils.

We describe the second type of loyalty to the nation as mundane nationalism. This type was clearly visible in the statements of the moderate nationalists, although some conformists also spoke in these terms. The teachers themselves described their attitude as 'modern patriotism' and opposed it – as they called it – to 'romantic patriotism', which emphasised the value of armed struggle and readiness to give up one's life. One of the teachers explained the basic principles of this 'modern patriotism': 'working honestly, taking part in general elections, being fair, not lying, paying taxes . . . this is not about throwing a grenade . . . to be an ordinary Polish citizen'. The teachers representing 'modern patriotism' criticised 'romantic patriotism' for focusing on armed struggle because it aroused hostility towards other nations, especially neighbouring ones:

> [T]he consequences of this will be that we don't like Russia, we don't like Ukraine . . . it can educate students to aversion to Russia. . ., and this is the biggest problem of education, civic education, that we have to build our sense of national belonging in such contrast to others . . . aversion to others.

However, this does not mean that there were no teachers among the moderate nationalists or conformists who did not think that sacrificing one's life as a nation is valuable. They believed, however, that, in the present peaceful times, there is no need to emphasise this dimension of nationalism: 'It'd be enough if we're honest and hardworking; I think that in peacetime, in this way, we can serve our homeland very well'.

Conclusion

In this chapter, we focused on the different types of nationalism represented by the teachers. The teachers differed mainly on four points: their understanding of the nation in the context of its inclusiveness, the importance that they attached to Polish history as opposed to general history, whether they focused on glorious events and figures or also took into account the dark sides of national history, and the patterns of loyalty to the nation that they promoted: the cult of armed struggle and sacrifice versus everyday ordinary duties. Thus, on the one hand, there is exclusive, Poland-first, uncritical, and militaristic nationalism; on the other hand, there is inclusive, international, critical, and mundane nationalism. The first type of nationalism was mainly typical of radical nationalists and the second of moderate nationalists. However, these types of nationalism have to be treated as ideal types in the Weberian sense as they have not always been 'pure' and cannot always be assigned unambiguously to a particular category of teachers (Swedberg, 2018). For example, the differences between the radical nationalists and the moderate nationalists were not clear cut: both types of teachers referred, for example, to glorious nationalism aimed at arousing national pride. In other words, exclusive, narcissistic, uncritical, and militaristic nationalism cannot be equated only with the radical nationalists because some moderate nationalists and above all some conformists also sometimes relied on this type of discourse and sometimes various teachers mixed the two types of nationalism. Finally, it must be recalled that this distinction of two types of nationalism does not include the opponents, who did not believe at all that the purpose of teaching history is to promote or strengthen national identity. They did not think in terms of what kind of nationalism schools should preach and instil in the pupils but stressed that they must teach about nationalism just as they teach about other ideologies, such as communism or Catholic fundamentalism.

References

Alter, P. (1994). *Nationalism*. London: Edward Arnold.
Bryan, A. (2009). The intersectionality of nationalism and multiculturalism in the Irish curriculum: Teaching against racism? *Race, Ethnicity and Education, 12*, 297–317.
Burszta, W. J., Dobrosielski, P., Jaskulowski, K., Majbroda, K., Majewski, P., & Rauszer, M. (2019). *Naród w szkole: Historia i nacjonalizm w polskiej edukacji szkolnej [The nation at school: History and nationalism in Polish school education]*. Gdańsk: Katedra.
Cadier, D., & Szulecki, K. (2020). Populism, historical discourse and foreign policy: The case of Poland's law and justice government. *International Politics, 57*, 990–1011.
Hein-Kircher, H. (2008). *Kult Piłsudskiego i jego znaczenie dla państwa polskiego 1926–1939 [The cult of Piłsudski and its significance for the Polish state, 1926–1939]*. Warszawa: Neriton.
Hutchins, R. D. (2011). Heroes and the renegotiation of national identity in American history textbooks: Representations of George Washington and Abraham Lincoln, 1982–2003. *Nations and Nationalism, 17*, 649–668.
Jaskulowski, K. (2003). *Mityczne przestrzenie nacjonalizmu [Mythical spaces of nationalism]*. Toruń: Adam Marszałek.
Jaskulowski, K. (2010). Western (civic) versus Eastern (ethnic) nationalism: The origins and critique of the dichotomy. *Polish Sociological Review, 171*, 289–303.
Jaskulowski, K. (2019). *The everyday politics of migration crisis in Poland: Between nationalism, fear and empathy*. Cham: Palgrave.
Jaskulowski, K., & Majewski, P. (2020). Politics of memory in upper Silesian schools: Between Polish homogeneous nationalism and its Silesian discontents. *Memory Studies, 13*(1), 60–73.
Jaskułowski, K., Majewski, P., & Surmiak, A. (2018). Teaching the nation: History and nationalism in Polish school history education. *British Journal of Sociology of Education, 39*(1), 77–91.
Kohn, H. (1944). *The idea of nationalism. A study in its origins and background*. New York: The Macmillan Company.
Kończal, K. (2020). The invention of the 'cursed soldiers' and its opponents: Postwar partisan struggle in contemporary Poland. *East European Politics and Societies, 34*(1), 67–95.
Kuzio, T. (2002). The myth of the civic state: A critical survey of Hans Kohn's framework for understanding nationalism. *Ethnic and Racial Studies, 1*, 20–39.

Kymlicka, W. (2001). *Politics in the vernacular: Nationalism, multiculturalism, and citizenship.* Oxford: Oxford University Press.

Porter, B. (2000). *When nationalism began to hate: Imagining modern politics in nineteenth century Poland.* Oxford: Oxford University Press.

Power, M. (1997). *The audit society: Rituals of verification.* Oxford: Oxford University Press.

Rüssen, J. (2004). Historical consciousness: Narrative structure, moral function and ontogenetic development. In P. Seixas (Ed.), *Theorizing historical consciousness* (pp. 63–85). Toronto: Toronto University Press.

Shibata, Y. (2013). *Discrimination for the sake of the nation: The discourse of the league of Polish families against 'others' 2001–2007.* Bern: Peter Lang.

Shore, C., & Wright, S. (2015). Governing by numbers: Audit culture, rankings and the new world order. *Social Anthropology, 23,* 22–28.

Swedberg, R. (2018). How to use Max Weber's ideal type in sociological analysis. *Journal of Classical Sociology, 18*(3), 181–196.

Walicki, A. (1994). *Philosophy and romantic nationalism: The case of Poland.* Notre Dame: University of Notre Dame Press.

Zubrzycki, G. (2006). *The crosses of Auschwitz: Nationalism and religion in postcommunist Poland.* Chicago: Chicago University Press.

5 Whose nation? Whose history?

Introduction

In previous chapters, we have demonstrated that the interviewed teachers generally defined the aims of historical education in nationalist terms. Although they, not counting the opponents, agreed on nationalist educational goals, they referred to various types of nationalism. In this chapter, we continue to analyse the differences between teachers by focusing on how their views on the nationalising of pupils translate into their teaching of history in the context of the representation of selected disadvantaged groups. We are interested in answering the question of what place in the canonical historical narrative teachers give to groups that have conventionally been marginalised in both historiography and public discourse in Poland. In other words, our aim is to explore the question of whose history teachers actually teach. This will allow us to deepen our understanding of the types of nationalism that Polish schools promote, especially in the context of inclusion/exclusion and power relations. We start our analysis in a broader context, namely exploring how teachers talk about the non-European world. Then, we focus on teachers' views on national minorities, women, and lower classes.

Europe and the rest

Both the core curriculum and the textbooks focus mainly on Polish history, which is presented in the context of the history of Europe and North America. The textbooks devote little space to the history of the non-European world, which is presented mainly in the context of colonisation and decolonisation processes. In addition, the non-European world, especially Africa and Australia, is represented in terms of Orientalist discourse as the binary opposite of European civilisation (Said, 1978). Africa, for example, is shown as a no-man's land, a continent without civilisation, or an unknown territory

DOI: 10.4324/9781003028529-5

that was just 'discovered' by Europeans. The textbooks describe Africans in essentialist terms as a homogeneous and savage population, devoid of any activity and living in a state of stagnation. European colonisation, however, is seen as a salutary event for Africa. Although the textbooks pay some attention to the darker sides of colonisation, such as wars and violence, slavery, and the economic exploitation, at the same time, they argue that it was only the Europeans who initiated the development of Africa and gave the natives the opportunity to emerge from a state of savagery and to embark on a path of progress (Burszta et al., 2019; Kalicińska, 2011).

In the textbooks, there are no echoes of the discussion on Eurocentrism and the legacy of colonialism that takes place in contemporary historical debates (Van Nieuwenhuyse, 2019; Van Nieuwenhuyse & Valentim, 2018). This is probably due to the fact that there is a widespread belief in Poland that the problem of colonialism and racism does not concern this country. Not only politicians and journalists but also historians and social researchers generally assume that Poland did not participate in the European colonial project, did not have overseas colonies, and did not create a colonial empire and is, therefore, free from racism (Balogun, 2018, 2020). Under these conditions, there has been no wider discussion of European colonialism and a need for a critical review of knowledge about non-European countries. This has also translated into the textbooks' content, which perpetuates the negative stereotypes of the non-European world. The interviewed teachers also did not pay much attention to the non-European world and generally saw no need to revise the textbooks. There were no major differences here between the radical nationalists, the conformists, and the moderate nationalists, which may reflect the widespread entrenchment of orientalising stereotypes in Poland. As one of the teachers said, 'there is a topic about colonialism . . . there was colonialism, trade, slavery, but I've the impression that this doesn't particularly concern us'.

Only a few teachers were critical of the representation of the non-European world in textbooks – some moderate nationalists and opponents. The former pointed to the domination of content concerning Poland and Europe:

> We're a little bit Eurocentric, there's a lot of Polish history, a little less history of Europe and almost no history of other continents, other civilizations, it practically doesn't happen in lower secondary school, unless there's a clash of European culture, European civilization with other civilizations, only then there are some mentions . . . only the history of one, single civilization is presented.

The opponents also considered historical education in Poland to be Eurocentric, but, unlike the moderate nationalists, they also looked for the reasons for this, seeing them in the low level of theoretical and methodological awareness of textbook and core curriculum authors. In their opinion, Eurocentrism is the result not only of traditional prejudices against the non-Western world but, above all, also of the facts that school education attaches very little importance to the teaching of history as a discipline and that pupils are not introduced to historians' disputes. For example, the opponents stressed that the textbooks do not discuss the post-colonial theory that undermines Western-centric narratives: 'completely ignored by textbooks is the whole post-colonial thread in historiography based on criticism of Euro-centric . . . concept of modernity . . . a certain concept of modernity that is posed as a definite model'. According to the opponents, the textbooks present the history of non-European countries in a stereotypical way, that is, in terms of modernisation understood as imitation of the West. As they argued, the textbooks do not consider at all the experience of the indigenous peoples as allegedly being without history.

Two discourses are evident in the other teachers' statements. Firstly, like the textbooks, the teachers focused on the so-called geographical discoveries and colonialism, which they constructed as a blessing for the colonised in line with 19th-century colonial discourse. They saw owning a colony as a source of pride and a source of wealth for the imperial powers. They spoke with admiration of imperial powers such as the United Kingdom, which managed the colonies well, spreading civilisation and progress. As one of the teachers said:

> We've talked about colonies recently, right, and someone asked why we didn't have colonies, right, as a country. It's presented that our specificity was a little different, comparing . . . someone asked why the British people are so wealthy, it's because of history, right.

These teachers' narratives about the non-Western world are shaped by the Orientalist discourse legitimising colonialism and imperialism (Hall, 1992; Said, 1978). To describe non-Western 'others', the teachers used colonial terminology and Western 'knowledge'. They generally viewed colonialism as a political and economic phenomenon but did not see it as a cultural phenomenon involving the construction of exotic images of a population conquered under the guise of objective knowledge. They reproduced the Orientalist discourse that presents colonial societies as backward, passive, and without any achievements, only needing to be 'discovered' and colonised by Europeans to escape from a state of stagnation.

However, some teachers pointed out the dark side of colonialism by talking, for example, about the rivalry between Western countries leading to wars and the economic exploitation of colonial societies, the effects of which these societies still suffer today. Nevertheless, they placed economic exploitation into the broader meta-narrative of modernisation, which, although it had its dark side, has brought civilisation to the colonised. They portrayed non-European societies as incapable of making the transition to modernity on their own. The teachers' statements echoed the 19th-century evolutionism with its concept of universal and objective linear progress from the so-called underdeveloped societies to highly developed ones. In the words of Immanuel Wallerstein (2006), it can be said that this is a manifestation of 'European universalism', assuming that the countries of the so-called 'West' set a model of development and progress for the rest of the world. By reproducing this discourse, the teachers silenced non-European experiences, and representations of other non-Western societies serve to build a sense of superiority based on the dichotomy between 'we', civilised people of the West, and 'they', savages deprived of civilisation.

Apart from colonial discourse, the second type of discourse, which can be described as a clash of civilisations, dominates the statements of the teachers (Huntington, 2011). In terms of the clash of civilisations, the teachers spoke mainly about Islam, which reflects the anti-Islamic prejudices that are widespread in Poland. This is how the radical nationalists, the conformists, and sometimes also the moderate nationalists spoke about Islam. Let us quote one of the radical nationalists, for example:

> We exaggerate with those values which have such a humanitarian, human dimension, we're supposed to make our pupils unusually positive about everything . . . e.g. we aren't supposed to say that Gypsies are lazy, and they actually are lazy . . . they don't work . . . they scrounge social benefits, they beg . . . in the name of this humanitarianism, such situations will arise . . . an Islamic caliphate, because sooner or later, in Germany or France, a situation will arise that they'll begin to slaughter each other, in Germany there're 3,000 mosques, in France there're 12 mln Arabs . . . politicians are stupid . . . they explain publicly that Islam is the religion of peace, but not Islam isn't the religion of peace, and it'd have to be shown cleverly by examples.

The teacher's statement reverberates with both Islamophobic and Romophobic themes, which are a manifestation of a broader trend in Polish society. Hegemonic Polishness is based on the exclusion of the Roma, who are defined as being radically different from and 'inferior' to 'us' Poles (Jaskulowski, 2019). In popular imaginary, a visible sign of this difference is the 'dark' colour of Roma people's skin, which is constructed as being incompatible with the assumed whiteness of Poles. Research on Islamophobia in Poland has shown that anti-Roma stereotypes are cast on Muslims, who are often identified with Arabs, who are also perceived through the prism of a darker skin complexion (Jaskulowski, 2019). Hegemonic images also construct Muslims as an existential threat to Poland and European civilisation (Bobako, 2017; Górak-Sosnowska & Pachocka, 2019; Pędziwiatr, 2017). The teacher's statement, presented earlier, fits into this Islamophobic discourse: he identified Muslims with Arabs and said that it is necessary to show pupils in history lessons that Islam is a religion that excludes peaceful coexistence with other religions and cultures.

Although these two discourses were dominant, some teachers tried to be critical of them. However, they were driven not so much by methodological or theoretical considerations as by practical ones. For example, there were Muslim children in the classroom, and the teachers began to wonder what they actually teach about Islam:

> There was the question of Islam, and there was one surah [in a textbook], it says about women that a Muslim can beat his wife if she disobeyed him, there was literally that surah quoted . . . and I had one Muslim girl in my class, and I didn't know how to approach it, because they read it there and I didn't know how to get out of it . . . it was put, very controversially, that Islam . . . was presented as so dangerous.

Such reflections are difficult to assign to one category of teachers. However, they were more typical of teachers from large cities, such as Warsaw, who have a greater chance of having pupils from minority and migrant cultures in their class. In such a context, even some radical nationalists were more cautious and began to wonder how, for example, to speak about Islam in a more neutral way.

Nation and national minorities

As we wrote earlier, the core curriculum and textbooks do not pay much attention to national minorities. The history of the homogeneous Polish nation is dominant, and the issue of minorities is presented from a Polish perspective. In contrast to the issue of the non-European world, teachers were more aware of the problem of representation of national minorities. This can be explained by three factors. Firstly, the issue of minorities was present in the public debate, especially during the period of democratic transformation as well as during Poland's accession to the European Union. There was a discussion on standards for the protection of minority rights, and, as a consequence, legal protection for selected minorities was introduced (Łodziński, 2005). Secondly, teachers as historians were aware that the Polish national identity is founded on the myth of a tolerant and multicultural Commonwealth (Davies, 1997). Thirdly, in the last years, the issue of the Jewish minority has also been widely discussed, especially in the context of Poles' participation in the Holocaust, which was triggered by the books of Jan Tomasz Gross (Dobrosielski, 2017). Briefly, unlike colonialism and imperialism, the issue of national minorities has been widely discussed and has been the subject of disputes between politicians and historians. When talking about minorities, many teachers have experienced an epistemic switch (Wansik, Akkerman, Zuiker, & Wubbels, 2018): they have become increasingly aware that there are many points of view and that the issue of minority representation is not obvious. The teachers, therefore, showed an interest in minorities, albeit to varying degrees and in different ways.

The conformists generally accepted the content of the core curriculum and textbooks and thought it was understandable that the textbooks focused on the Polish nation, defined as a homogeneous community. They believed that the textbooks paid sufficient attention to minorities: 'I think that as much as is in the textbook is enough. There is no need to expand on it'. Not only did the conformists believe that the core curriculum and textbooks devote sufficient space to minorities, but they also accepted the way in which minorities are presented. As one of the conformists explained, 'as far as the representation of national and ethnic minorities is concerned, it is adequately presented in this textbook'. The conformists reproduced the homogenising discourse of traditional Polish nationalism, which largely marginalises minorities. Even if they mentioned minorities, their presence was used instrumentally to show the tolerance of the Polish nation, especially in modern times, in accordance with the myth of a state without stakes dominating the Polish collective memory (Davies, 1997). Minorities were also used to demonstrate the differences between 'us' and 'them': if the conformists spoke of minorities, they did so in terms of essentialised 'others' representing strangeness. For example, the Jews embody an exotic alienation, the Ukrainians represent a different, by implication backward, eastern civilisation, while the Germans and Russians embody hostility and danger. In other words, the conformists reproduced textbook strategies to reinforce the vision of hegemonic homogeneity. They reproduced the dominant 'Pole–Catholic' narrative, which leaves little room for minorities unless they assimilate with the titular nation. They took such a Polonocentric vision for granted. They also avoided talking about conflicts, focusing primarily on the unity of the Polish nation (Burszta et al., 2019).

The radical nationalists took a different stance: they believed that there is generally too much about minorities in the textbooks, especially about the Jews. They noted that minorities cannot be ignored; they must be mentioned, for example, to show that Poles have always accepted them, if only the minorities remembered that they are guests and have adapted to the rules prevailing in Poland. In general, however, the radical nationalists held the view that there is not much space and time to devote more attention to minorities. They believed that Polish schools are not a good place to present the minorities' perspectives on disputed issues. On the contrary, Polish schools should promote the Polish viewpoint. In their opinion, the textbooks are unfortunately often too pro-minority. For example, one of the radical nationalists defended the ethnic cleansing of Ukrainians, Lemkos, and Boykos undertaken by the communists in 1947 (Motyka, 2011):

> I've the impression that not all aspects of this Operation Vistula are shown. Because there's only about brutality . . . but there isn't any mention of helplessness . . . I try to show that, when fighting the Ukrainian partisans, they used a method which was supposed to destroy the partisans by cutting them off from their background, and the partisans' background was Ukrainian civilians . . . they were farmers in everyday life, only at night they went to fight . . . they underwent the Operation Vistula because they had no other idea how to solve it.

The quotation not only indicates an aversion to the 'pro-minority' narrative of the textbooks but also reveals a certain paradox. Although the radical nationalists usually presented themselves as anti-communists, the actions of the communists, leading to the construction of an ethnically homogeneous state, often met with their approval.

As we have already noted, in the opinion of the radical nationalists, Poland was generally a victim, and national honour did not allow the Poles to be aggressors – the same applies to internal politics. The radical nationalists stressed that, if Poles took any action against minorities, it was generally in self-defence, as was the case with the aforementioned Operation Vistula. They tended to deny that Poles or the Polish state discriminated against minorities. On the contrary, in their opinion, Poles have always shown hospitality. As one of the radical nationalists explained:

> Our history needs to be debunked. I can give concrete examples . . . the issue of the Jews. The textbook should convey one message, that through the ages we had a state in which the Jews found a second home. They couldn't stand living with anti-Semites for centuries. So I think that what is claimed, that we're anti-Semites . . . obviously there are such incidents, episodes, but it wasn't a rule. The Jews chose Poland as a second homeland . . . if there hadn't been the Holocaust, Poland would still have been their second homeland. . . . I don't agree that

we're anti-Semites. I think that the textbooks should show that neighbourhood relations [Polish – Jewish] were exemplary. And the fact that there were national problems in the interwar period was a certain aspect of the tide of nationalism, which was born on the wave of crisis. And these problems were everywhere, in both the USA and Russia, and in Western Europe, of which Hitler is the best example.

Paradoxically, the teacher spoke of debunking history, but he idealised Polish history by denying that Poles were anti-Semites (Jaskulowski & Majewski, 2020). He constructed anti-Semitism as a temporary phenomenon, caused by the extraordinary circumstances of the economic crisis and not specific to Poland. It is quite characteristic that, when talking about minorities, he also treated them in terms of a problem (in Polish, the word 'problem' also means trouble), which was also typical of some conformists and moderate nationalists.

The moderate nationalists, in general, criticised the core curriculum and textbooks for not giving enough space to minorities. They argued that more needs to be said about minorities, because students know little about them and hold various negative stereotypes about, for example, Jews or Germans.

> They come with a lot of stereotypes, prejudices. . . . I'll give you an example. . . . I had a lesson about Judaism. And when the term Jews appeared, the comments were unbelievable. I asked: 'do you know who they are? Do you know anything about them?' . . . The kids don't know, but they're anti-Jewish.

The moderate nationalists believed that textbooks are of little use here because they devote little space to cultural diversity: 'I've to admit that these themes of multiculturalism are a little bit lost in serious politics, in serious history'. In their opinion, the textbooks, for political reasons, reinforce the image of a homogeneous Polish nation: 'generally speaking, the pattern of a Pole–Catholic is reproduced, which is very bad'. As another teacher explained in more detail:

> This is ideologised . . . on the one hand, we're happy that Poland was multinational, and on the other hand, in the course of three years there's just one theme about the multicultural mosaic. And a child in an upper secondary school has no chance of finding out, for example, who the Jews were.

The moderate nationalists in this context aimed to develop what could be described as critical consciousness among schoolchildren, so, in this case, they challenged the hegemonic stereotypical views of a homogeneous Polish nation (Rüssen, 2004). As one moderate nationalist elucidated:

> The historian's task is to fight against such harmful, destructive myths, for example a Pole–Catholic . . . historian should probably deconstruct it a bit when it comes to religious identity, because it is awfully based on myths . . . that's what children should learn from history. . . . I think that a lot has been done recently on the Jewish subject . . . it doesn't have to be such a priority anymore . . . but still not much is said about Polish Orthodox Christians, Calvinists, Lutherans.

In the opinion of the moderate nationalists, it is important to denounce not only auto-stereotypes, such as the Pole–Catholic one, but also stereotypes about other nations. For example, one moderate nationalist explained how he modifies the textbook in the context of Polish–Ukrainian relations:

> Relations with Ukrainians . . . simplifications 'A Ukrainian is a Communist' . . . 'a Ukrainian is a Nazi', looking at Ukrainians . . . as exclusively UPA soldiers, such things happen . . . I wouldn't expect the textbook . . . I mean, there're such things, but it's really a task for the teacher to explain it fairly objectively and to show that Poles are partly guilty of this situation when it comes to Polish–Ukrainian relations.

The moderate nationalists criticised the textbooks not only for the fact that they portray minorities in a stereotypical way but also for presenting only the Polish point of view. In the case of national minorities, the moderate nationalists were in favour of using a certain degree of multiperspectivity, although they did not use the term (Stradling, 2003; Wansik et al., 2018).

> There are some mentions in the textbook about the attitudes towards minorities, but this is a tiny thing, there are some about Ukraine, because there are many fights there, that there're very many Jews. However, when it comes to these conflicts with the Ukrainians, it's always the case that we're right. . . . But it's not the case that some people are very good and others aren't.

However, this multiperspectivity has its limits. The moderate nationalists believed that minorities were worth presenting and celebrating if they showed loyalty to the Polish state. As one moderate nationalist explained, 'Children should learn from history that there were, or are, great Polish Lutheran and Orthodox patriots'. They spoke about minorities in terms of a kind of 'nationalist multiculturalism' (Hutchins, 2016, p. 62). In other words, if minorities demonstrated Polish patriotism, they were 'good' minorities. The moderate nationalists also tended, like the textbooks, to portray minorities as others or 'guests', existing for the benefit of the dominant nation. Thus, they still spoke about minorities in terms of objectified otherness; minorities were seen as outsiders who exist for the benefit of the dominant group (Bryan, 2009). Teachers noted, for example, that minorities enrich the Polish national culture by diversifying its cuisine or introducing some 'exotic' clothing. One could say that they spoke about minorities in terms of boutique multiculturalism, which does not require fundamental changes and negotiation of cultural differences (Fish, 1997; Jaskulowski, 2019). Minorities that could not fit into this 'positive' pattern of nationalist and boutique multiculturalism were regarded as 'bad' minorities, for example the Roma, stigmatised by many teachers: 'I don't know what it's like with Gypsies, because they've this specificity, they're so demanding, such a bit, they seem dirty, disgusting, nasty, they're so suspicious, right?'

However, some moderate nationalists have broken out of this pattern of boutique and nationalist multiculturalism, especially teachers from national minorities. For example, teachers who defined themselves as Silesians said that the problem is not only that textbooks do not give enough space to minorities but also that the whole historical narrative is written from the Warsaw perspective (Jaskulowski & Majewski, 2020). This 'Warsaw history' – as they called it – does not take into account the specificity of border areas inhabited by minorities, such as Upper Silesia. Interestingly, the term 'Warsaw history' was also used by some radical nationalists, who also criticised textbooks for not taking into account the experiences of other regions. The radical nationalists, however, stated that the textbooks paid too little attention to the traditions of fighting for Polishness in the peripheral regions of Poland. For example, one of the radical nationalists criticised the marginalisation of the Wielkopolska Uprising of 1918–1919:

> It's there that the Wielkopolska won, but it wasn't nationwide, so it's local, so only a small part of the space is devoted to it. . . . But in the end Poznań is as good as . . . as an important centre of Polishness, because in the end it's the cradle of Polish statehood, as Cracow or Warsaw, so why should it be treated worse? However, this Warsaw, Warsaw point of view is very strong.

However, the moderate nationalists from Upper Silesia placed less emphasis on the fact that the textbooks did not show the tradition of fighting for Polishness in other more peripheral regions of Poland but highlighted that the textbooks omit everything that does not fit into the dominant concept of Polishness. For example, the textbooks say very little about Poland's links with German-speaking countries or the influence of German culture on Poland. This is because it does not fall within the concept of hegemonic Polishness, built on opposition to Germany. In their opinion, however, it is precisely the links with Germany that have been of key importance to the history of Upper Silesia. That is why they believed that the history of these regions, and of Upper Silesia in particular, is shown in a deformed way for political reasons (Jaskulowski & Majewski, 2020).

The Silesian teachers admitted that they use their autonomy to modify the content of curricula and textbooks. Symptomatically, they spoke about it rather hesitantly. They had to be assured that the interviews were anonymous and their identity would not be revealed. They said that there was pressure from politicians and local authorities on teachers to teach according to the curriculum. They feared not only their own position but also that of the interviewer. For example, one of the teachers warned the researcher: 'but don't even write it down, because someone in Warsaw may destroy you'. The teachers' fear was due to the living memory of the persecution of and discrimination against Silesians by the Polish state in the interwar period and after 1945 (Woźniczka, 2010). This period is remembered as the 'Upper Silesian Tragedy' among Silesians. Many Silesians who were classified as Germans were expelled from Poland, while others were Polonised (e.g. officials changed their local names to something more Polish). Interestingly, when some teachers talked about this period, they used the phrase 'those Poles who came here' and the pronoun 'us', that is, Silesians, as opposed to 'them', Poles (Jaskulowski & Majewski, 2020). This mistrust of the Polish state is aggravated by the fact that the Polish state does not recognise Silesians as a national or ethnic minority. Moreover, right-wing politicians stigmatise the Silesian minority and those Silesian activists who talk about autonomy, accusing them of being crypto-Germans who want to join Upper Silesia with Germany (Jaskulowski, 2012).

The teachers were afraid because they teach about Upper Silesia in a way that undermines the hegemonic collective memory. Thus, one of the teachers explained how his teaching extends beyond textbooks:

> They [the students] go to lower secondary school and have contact with a teacher like me who says, no, it is not so, the history is different. In the Battle of Grunwald, our knights fought on the side of the Teutonic Knights. Silesian uprisings do not have to be called national uprisings but rather civil wars . . . and there is a lesson on the origins of Slavic states, so I tell children about Silesian tribes, that this word [Silesia] does not have to come from Silesian but from the tribe Silings.

Thus, this teacher undermines three points of the Polish national interpretation of history: that the name Silesia comes from the Slavic language; that the Battle of Grunwald was, in fact, more complex than is suggested by Polish nationalist imagination, which presents it as a great victory for Poles over Germany; and that the Silesian uprisings were civil wars because the Silesians were divided and fought on both sides of the conflict, Polish and German. Let us note that the teacher called the medieval knights 'ours' by constructing an ahistorical Silesian entity separate from the Polish one (Jaskulowski & Majewski, 2020).

However, the Silesian teachers paid most attention to the Second World War in the specific context of Upper Silesia. This period was crucial to them, which can be explained by the fact that the war had enormous consequences for Upper Silesia. Moreover, by teaching about this period, they and their pupils can also draw on the living memory of the witnesses. In other words, they referred to 'communicative memory' as opposed to institutionalised school cultural memory (Assmann, 2011). Stories based on the living memory of Silesians are often critical of the Polish state:

> When I teach about the Second World War . . . the grandparents are still alive . . . my mother-in-law when the war began, she was a teenager . . . and she remembers something that is not taught in history classes. You know, as Germans entered, the people greeted them with flowers. . . . I mention to the children about it. I don't know if I do right or wrong, but history should tell things as they actually were, and in the textbook they do not find that.
>
> (Interview 5)

In this case, the memories not only are critical of the Polish state but also break the Polish national taboo. The teacher suggested that some Silesians were waiting for the Germans in 1939 because they thought they would be better off in Nazi Germany than in Poland. Another teacher tells children about his grandfather, who volunteered for the Wehrmacht: his grandfather was warned by a friend who worked in the administration that he would be conscripted and sent to the eastern front in Russia. His grandfather decided to volunteer for the Wehrmacht, because in that case he thought he could choose which front he wanted to go to, so he chose the Western Front because he believed that he had a better chance of surviving there. However, serving in the Wehrmacht army does not fit into the dominant national collective memory. Similarly, the textbooks treat as traitors those Poles who signed the Deutsche Volksliste (German National List):

> There [in the textbook] is an entire entry on the Volksliste; as I tell the pupils, it's such a Warsaw-centred perspective, so Polonocentric, all of

them were traitors; there's such a condemnation of these people who signed the list and I always ask the students where their grandparents were during the Second World War, maybe here.

However, as the Silesian teachers reminded us, in occupied Upper Silesia, former Polish citizens were forced to sign this list under threat of deportation to a concentration camp. The Silesian teachers, therefore, practised a critical history that undermined certain elements of the hegemonic historical narrative, which they considered to be biased. They presented their narrative as true, understanding historical truth in a specific way. For them, true history seems to be a history that is based on the living memories of people who witnessed past events (Jaskulowski & Majewski, 2020). They were united with other moderate nationalists by the fact that they excluded their own narrative from critical scrutiny, presenting it as unambiguously true.

The opponents paradoxically resembled conformists at first sight. They believed that relatively much is said about minorities in Polish schools:

> Minorities appear in the curriculum . . . this is a new group that has received some attention . . . Polish–Ukrainian relations . . . or Jewish minority. . . . It has already been recognised at some point that . . . it's impossible to teach the history of the Second Polish Republic . . . without this anti-Semitism, a minority background.

However, they differed from the conformists in two respects. Firstly, according to the opponents, although the textbooks mention minorities, they continue to present a traditional vision of history, focused primarily on the narrowly understood Polish nation. Minority topics are only a supplement and are not accompanied by any systematic change in the approach to history that would take many different perspectives seriously. According to the opponents, the modifications are often superficial and based on a commonsense approach:

> Very often I've seen such a concept like let's keep the balance . . . let's say something good, then let's say something bad . . . lets us complicate it, it's the way that you try to settle disputed issues in Poland . . . and it also seems to everyone that the balance means that we say something bad about both sides, and then it will be good, and that the truth lies right in the middle. It doesn't.

Secondly, the opponents underlined that textbooks devote a relatively large amount of space to minorities – but only when compared with the coverage of other underprivileged groups, such as women and the popular classes.

Their comments that there is relatively much about minorities in the textbooks must be seen in this context. Thus, although the opponents may seem less critical of the way in which minorities are portrayed in the textbooks than the moderate nationalists, especially the Silesian ones, this is because they looked at the textbooks from a broader perspective. It should also be remembered that the opponents, in general, rejected the nationalist framework of history as given and self-evident and did not look at minorities from the Polonocentric point of view. They also differed from other teachers in their epistemological approach: they were not particularly looking for a single historical truth – they did not want to replace one narrative with another one that was allegedly better and more true – but they emphasised the perspectivity of every piece of historical knowledge, including their own.

Nation and gender

Since its beginning, nationalism has been part of the ideology of hegemonic masculinity (Connell, 2005; Mosse, 1988; Nagel, 1998; Yuval-Davis & Anthias, 1989). The emerging nation states were dominated by men who monopolised positions of power, prestige, and wealth. The dominant culture of masculinity normalised the division into 'better' male roles and 'worse' female social roles. The ideology of nationalism strengthened the position of men by defining a nation as a community of brotherhood, a community of men whose natural role is to deal with public affairs and defend national borders. Nationalism involves empowerment of broad masses, hypothetically creating the possibility for women to take on new social roles other than those assigned to them by pre-modern societies. In practice, however, nationalist movements have not so much led to equal rights for women as made them disempowered icons of nationalist ideology. Women began to function in a double symbolic role: as allegories of a nation (a nation as a woman) and as the embodiment of its identity, borders, and honour (a woman as a nation). Women were charged with the burden of representing national honour, their civil rights were restricted, and they were pushed away from active participation in public life, their social roles being mainly confined to the biological and cultural reproduction of the nation (Nagel, 1998).

From the beginning of its history, Polish nationalism has also granted men a privileged position. Polish nationalism glorified the male relationship portrayed by means of the metaphor of brotherhood – friendship. This imaginary union embraced a series of male generations fighting and killing for the nation: medieval knights and rulers, noble leaders, 19th-century insurgents, legionnaires, Second World War soldiers, Warsaw insurgents, and, more recently, cursed soldiers. This male community has been depicted in national poetry, fiction, painting, and history books. The nationalist sacralisation of male communities was accompanied by the idealisation of femininity, which was reflected in the sanctified figure of the mother represented by one of the central Polish national religious symbols, Our Lady of Czestochowa. In Polish hegemonic nationalist ideology, women were reduced to the symbolic role of representatives of the national cause and the cultural and biological reproducers of the nation. Women were to deal with the private sphere, and their participation in public life was to be limited to secondary roles consistent with the alleged female 'nature' (Kurczewska, 1999; Walczewska, 2000).

The core curriculum and school textbooks fall into this hegemonic masculine and male-centric nationalist discourse, telling the history of the nation mainly through the prism of men's achievements. Regarding the teachers' view on women in history, there were some differences between them, but they did not entirely coincide with the categories of teachers that we have identified. The majority of the teachers turned out to be conformists, who did not consider the issue of women's representation to be problematic. For example, one of the teachers, when asked about the representation of women, explained, 'There is no separate topic like a woman in history, it can be done during History and Society course . . . how a woman is presented in history, whether she is presented depends on the teacher and this is how it should be'. The lack of greater interest in the issue may testify to the strength of the patriarchal concept of the nation; it may also be due to the fact that teachers are attached to the Rankian model of history focused on narrowly understood political history as a collection of political facts: the deeds of politicians, statesmen, the military, and activists.

This does not mean, of course, that no teachers raised the subject of women. Some radical nationalists took a firm stand: they associated the issue of women with 'genderism' and feminism, which they saw as dangerous because it undermines the traditional social order. The radical nationalists believed that gender is of little importance in history: 'there's no such thing in the textbooks as to specifically expose this or that gender, because, in fact, why? Why should gender be a determining factor?' The teacher praised the textbooks for being gender neutral and for not exposing the issue. However, he was de facto reproducing in this way, under the guise of objectivity, the masculine-centred concept of history. At the same time, however, the same teacher said that he sometimes likes to swim against the current and expose the role of women in history. As he explained, 'I sometimes like to stir up the pot and I show that the Middle Ages, for example, wasn't as masculinised as we think, that women played a huge role there . . . but again I don't focus on it'. The teacher's approach was quite typical of some radical nationalists, who sometimes exposed the role of women if they could be incorporated into political history and performed the functions traditionally played by men, for example, a ruler. For the radical nationalists, this occasional male role of women was not so much a challenge to the traditional order as proof that there was no patriarchalism in European history. The radical nationalists not only constructed the past primarily in terms of men's history but also saw history as a subject that is and should be of interest mainly to boys. In their view, history as a tale of wars and great politics is primarily aimed at boys: it shows them the exemplary male roles of national heroes whom the boys should admire.

The moderate nationalists, however, tended to emphasise that the textbooks pay too little attention to women. In their opinion, topics devoted to women offer a good opportunity to introduce the issue of gender equality to pupils. As one moderate nationalist explained:

> There isn't much of this content . . . it has only been around for a few years, and I think it is probably thanks to non-governmental organisations . . . to put emphasis on such feminist or simply gender equality content. Poles are only just beginning to talk about this and the whole affair with the so-called 'gender' is proof of this.

The teacher referred to 'the affair', making an allusion to right-wing rhetoric aimed at causing moral panic over gender, which is presented as an ideology of 'genderism' threatening the traditional Polish and Catholic family (Szwed & Zielińska, 2017). The teacher suggested that the gender issues that he identifies with gender equality are relatively new in Poland and are not taken into account in the curricula. Symptomatically, the teacher emphasised the role of NGOs, and other teachers wishing to include gender issues also often stressed that they receive assistance from NGOs, which provide them with various materials, because there is little in the textbooks on the subject. Thus, some moderate nationalists use their autonomy to supplement textbooks and introduce gender content into teaching: 'I myself try to show it . . . these themes appear but there are few; there could be more'.

The moderate nationalists reported that they use history lessons to talk about gender equality, which can be described in terms of developing aimed critical historical consciousness in pupils (Rüssen, 2004). Their understanding of gender equality was characterised by three points. Firstly, they defined equality primarily in legal and political terms as equal rights for men and women. Secondly, they inscribed the issue of gender equality into a meta-narrative about the progress and improvement of the legal and political situation of women in Europe. The moderate nationalists constructed gender inequality primarily as a historical problem that existed in the past. In their opinion, in contemporary Europe, the problem of inequality has been resolved and the question of guaranteeing equal rights for women is now primarily a matter for less developed countries. Thirdly, they also highlighted Poland's historical achievements in introducing equal rights. As one moderate nationalist noted, 'I always say that Poland was one of the first countries to grant rights to women, as early as 1918'.

On the one hand, the moderate nationalists criticised the textbooks and stressed that there could be more about women. On the other hand, the moderate nationalists inscribed women into a traditional nationalist historical narrative, emphasising above all their contribution to the fight for independence:

> There are themes that are developed now, but not at school, outside the school, such as Women on the war front, Women in the Uprisings, in this Warsaw Uprising. These are things beyond the curriculum, of course, if the teachers want to, if they are aware that it is important, they can do it.

In other words, the moderate nationalists believed that women are important as long as they fit into a traditional nationalist historical narrative. Therefore, the moderate nationalists criticised the core curriculum and textbooks for not having enough content on women, but at the same time they did not see the need for any more profound revision of the approach to history in textbooks. They would like to have more on women in the textbooks but mainly within the framework of the existing concept of history.

The opponents, especially women, were more critical. They defined gender inequality in broader terms than moderate nationalism since they also included a question of cultural power and believed that women and men were far from fully empowered. The opponents strongly criticised the textbooks and the core curriculum. As one of the opponents said, 'I cooperate with some feminist NGOs, I made an analysis of the core curriculum, I took such a feminist look at it, and it's really, say, quite terrible'. The opponents stressed the need for change, but they explained that it is not enough to include more themes about women in the textbooks, stating that there must be deeper modification of the very concept of school history, 'not just that there should be more women in history textbooks . . . this requires some fundamental change in thinking about how history should be taught and what it actually is'. The opponents argued that a greater number of female characters in the textbooks, if they are shown in stereotypical roles, will not change anything or may even perpetuate the hegemonic images of femininity as subordinated to masculinity. As one of the teachers explained, there is no female perspective in the textbooks:

> [T]hese textbooks aren't designed to allow us to see and talk about the role of women in this masculine world, much more masculine than

today. . . . I often ask children to deliver presentations or papers about women. . . . Research has been carried out that during the Crusades women in the West stayed at home and took care of property, and then their role increased. It seems to me that there's one sentence about this in one of these textbooks, but I won't give a damn. In any case, it's more so that women appear in everyday life as a curiosity . . . how women were dressed.

In the opinion of the opponents, women are presented mainly as an addition to the male world in contexts that are considered to be of little importance and in line with the stereotypical image of women as being focused on their appearance and the private sphere. The opponents also considered that the textbooks pay too little attention to gender inequality in the past:

> History is actually written without women . . . the student will not even find out that women once didn't have the right to vote . . . there is no such topic, right. And it's also so striking, of course in some textbooks it usually looks better, yeah, there're some chapters devoted to emancipation in the past, the 19th century . . . in the case of Poland, of course, to women in various independence movements.

While the moderate nationalists took for granted the liberal meta-narrative of the constant improvement of the situation of women in Europe, the opponents rejected it as simplified. They believed that this narrative ignores women's efforts and struggle for equality, presenting the achievement of equal rights as an inevitable process of steady progress or the result of men's decisions. In their opinion, this narrative also obscures the fact that the position of women in European societies is still not equal.

According to the opponents, this lack of a female perspective in the core curriculum is due to the 'patriarchal concept of the nation'. They pointed out that school history is focused on the history of the Polish nation, which is defined in masculine categories as a community of men dealing with public affairs. Women in this community perform subordinate and socially less respected functions that are hidden in the private sphere and considered to be of little historical importance. Thus, the contestants also pointed out the second reason for the lack of a female perspective, namely the anachronistic concept of history: 'The problem is that . . . the entire core curriculum, with such a tiny exception of this module History and Society . . . is completely anachronistic. . . . [T]here's only political history . . . the state and the nation . . . there are mostly men'. As she further explained:

> The way the land was cultivated in the 13th century isn't historically important, or the number of women who died during childbirth isn't

historically important either . . . school history creates hierarchies of importance . . . there're important battles . . . great politics, men and there're those other things that aren't important that don't deserve a place in a textbook.

The opponents, in the context of women, not only drew attention to the critical functions of history, which was also characteristic of the moderate nationalists, but also pointed to the need to rethink the entire history curriculum. They called for a more disciplinary approach to history, rejecting narrowly understood political history and including topics inspired by history from below and by women's history. This would not only allow the inclusion of more women in textbooks but also give pupils a better understanding of the past, which cannot be reduced to the history of wars and battles.

Nation and class

Nationalism assumes that a nation is the main object of identification and the basis of collective solidarity, which has priority over other forms of social identity. Nationalism constructs a nation as a harmonious community that is often represented by the metaphor of the family or home. Even if there are conflicts between groups within a nation, they are constructed as temporary and secondary and, in extreme cases, as inspired by external or internal enemies as a nation is imagined as an inherently cohesive community (Anderson, 1991). However, nationalist discourse does not function in a social vacuum: in today's complex societies, there are other discourses that organise human identity. In this section, we are interested in the problem of class representation and economic inequality in the context of the history of the Polish nation. It is worth adding here that the core curriculum speaks of developing the social sensitivity of pupils. However, in the core curriculum and in the textbooks, the issue of economic inequality occupies a marginal place in comparison with the narrowly understood political history focused on the struggle of the Polish nation against internal and external enemies (Jaskulowski & Surmiak, 2017). The interviewed teachers also did not pay much attention to the issues of inequality and class conflict, yet there were some differences between them.

The radical nationalists associated class divisions with the Marxist concept of class struggle, which they, in turn, identified with communist or even Stalinist propaganda. They claimed that the concept of class struggle deformed social reality, of which the basic and fundamental elements are harmonious and coherent nations. In their view, there are inequalities between different groups within a nation, but these inequalities cannot be described in terms of a class struggle for two reasons. Firstly, according to the radical nationalists, class itself is a discredited Marxist idea; there are people with different economic statuses but that does not determine their identity and interests. Secondly, inequalities between groups never take such an extreme form as the Marxists and pre-1989 textbooks described, and economic differences are of secondary importance in a shared national belonging. Let us quote one of the teachers:

> What class conflicts? Jesus Christ, what kind of nomenclature is this? Class conflict, it's an era of deep Stalinism. There aren't any class conflicts. Where do these questions come from? I'm very sorry, I'm embarrassed. What kind of conflicts . . . division into classes, well, I think we've already dealt with them and no longer, there are no class conflicts . . . we know that there're inequalities, they're somehow shown in different epochs.

Some radical nationalists even underestimated the economic inequalities in history: 'these issues aren't specifically discussed . . . there's surely some mention of it, but whether there's an emphasis on social inequality, I'd say no . . . it's a good textbook'. However, other radical nationalists sometimes criticised the textbooks for paying too much attention to this issue. For example, one of the radical nationalists answered the question about how class conflicts are presented in textbooks: 'this question is a bit communist. . . . I think there's actually still, such a pro-left-wing approach [in textbooks]'. Interestingly, some radical nationalists worked in schools in impoverished cities, which are still experiencing a structural economic and social crisis caused by the shock economic therapy introduced by economically neoliberal governments after 1989. The teachers were aware of poverty and pauperisation because they noticed that many students cannot afford to buy new textbooks. Some teachers admitted in the interviews that they violated copyright law and photocopied textbooks for students whose parents could not afford them: 'there's a lot of unemployment, and buying a textbook is a problem. . . . We make photocopies, although I know it is illegal' (Jaskulowski & Surmiak, 2017). However, this awareness of poverty and social problems did not influence the teachers' approach to history. In other words, they did not look at history from the lower classes' point of view and did not stress their agency or interests but constructed the past in terms of elite history.

This reluctance to discuss social class at school can be explained by several factors. We have already mentioned that the radical nationalists defined history in Rankian terms as a history of wars, battles, and great politics.

They marginalised social history and the activity of the lower social classes. Teachers also claimed that the pupils themselves were mainly interested in political history. As one of the teachers explained:

> The Second World War . . . the fronts . . . the political situation . . . the USSR's attacks on our lands, they love these subjects, and the boys especially. Well, totalitarianisms are very cool, the creation of the Soviet Union, the uprisings, Nazi Germany, Fascist Italy, all this is of interest to them, but if we start to get into culture or economy . . . then it's just terrible.

We also noted that the radical nationalists spoke of a lack of 'patriotism' among schoolchildren, which they associated with the crisis of a traditional family. In their opinion, the school should counteract this and instil in the pupils an attachment to the nation. Paradoxically, the teachers' awareness of the difficult social and economic situation in which their pupils find themselves does not prompt them to highlight social tensions in history and develop social sensitivity among their pupils; instead, they underestimate or omit these problems in their teaching. In their view, highlighting the importance of social conflicts poses a threat to the idea of an ideologically united and homogeneous nation. In a word, teaching about classrooms and class conflicts can even destabilise the national-centric logic of historical education. Some radical nationalists believed that social or economic history, in general, is of little use because it is not suitable for conveying the most desirable values, that is, national values.

The conformists took a similar position to that of radical nationalists, although they spoke about class struggle with a less emotional tone. For them, it was the domain of pre-1989 teaching and, therefore, they treated it with some antipathy. They thought that social conflicts and social inequalities were sufficiently covered by the textbooks: 'There're mentions about it in the context of a given nation . . . throughout history, from ancient times, from Egypt to Rome . . . the rights of people . . . about peasants a lot, about the nobility'. The conformists saw no need for special emphasis on social issues and class inequalities and looked at them, especially in the Polish history context, from the perspective of the formation of a 'fully fledged' nation comprising all social groups. Let us explain this with an example:

- How are social and class inequalities represented?
- Attention is drawn to the fact that the nobility was a nation . . . that is, our nation consisted of 10% of the population, it was a nation and the rest was beyond the definition. Of course, the peasants' situation is highlighted, and so on, and how these nobles were granted further

privileges . . . what an undesirable impact this had on the development of our society, that is, the limited role of the king, the fact that they [nobles] took advantage of their position, because this was mainly about peasants, right . . . when peasants gained national consciousness, actually in the only the 19th century.

When asked about a class conflict, a teacher stated that the nobility oppressed peasants and misused its power, which delayed the peasants' acquisition of national awareness. The conformists saw social history as a background for understanding the formation of the nation, as the mere context for various important events in national history, such as the failed uprisings in the 19th century. Therefore, once again, we are dealing with a nation-centred logic of historical education, in which social history serves nationalist educational purposes:

> There are social issues in the history lessons. . . . It's impossible to explain the reasons for the defeat of this failed uprising of 1846 without discussing the reasons that led to the outbreak of the Peasant Uprising of 1846. Here, not only Austria's actions but above all the issue of social differences and social inequalities mattered.

The conformists, like the radical nationalists, also believed that the pupils themselves were not very interested in social history. At the same time, the conformists pointed out that it is hard to teach about social class because, for the pupils, it is an outdated concept: 'for them, class inequality is a completely distant concept; they live in a world where it is difficult to talk about such a rigid class division as it was one hundred years ago'. Teachers construct students as having difficulties in understanding the notion of a social class, but they themselves increase these difficulties by defining the class as a 19th-century notion, which is useless today because contemporary Polish society lacks clear class divisions. The conformists associated class and class conflict mainly with the early days of industrialisation when workers were deprived of any social security and were only beginning to fight for their social and political rights. In this way, the conformists routinely submitted to the neoliberal discourse that prevailed in Poland after 1989 and that has eliminated the notion of class from the public debate for not fitting with the contemporary individualised society, in which our social and economic status allegedly depends only on our work and effort (Markiewka, 2017).

Interestingly, the moderate nationalists also did not want to be linked to Marxism, and they associated the concept of class with Marxism, which they identified not with social theory but with the communist political system:

'The motif of class conflicts is very unfashionable at the moment. . . . It's, by the way, the most common theme in the 19th century, but Marxism is rather avoided'. The moderate nationalists also focused on political history but paid more attention to social and economic factors in history than the radical nationalists and conformists. They treated social and economic issues as the background necessary to explain political phenomena and processes. When talking about social inequalities and class conflicts, the moderate nationalists focused mainly on two issues. Firstly, they stressed that the core curriculum and textbooks do not pay sufficient attention to the peasants. Such opinions may partially reflect the debate initiated by left-wing activists and some academics on the marginalisation of peasants in the Polish collective memory (Leszczyński, 2020; Rauszer, 2020). As one of the moderate nationalists stated:

> We're a peasant nation, which took over the culture of the nobility . . . unfortunately, the culture of the nobility in its worst dimension, the Sarmatian one, there's no such thing as a folk culture, there's . . . there is no such thing as a bourgeois culture, there is no such thing at all. . . . There is only noble culture, I'm talking about this textbook.

Another moderate nationalist criticised the textbooks in a similar vein:

> I've never actually seen the peasants' point of view. If the theme of peasants appears at all, it's rather when it [the textbook] describes the enfranchisement of peasants. . . . But then it can always put into this context 'our poor peasants, those partitioners oppressed them' because at that time Poland was partitioned, so not Poles versus Poles at all but poor Polish peasants versus partitioners. I've never seen there anything about class divisions, any emphasis on them.

According to the moderate nationalists, not only are there too few themes on peasants but also the textbooks do not take the peasant perspective into account. Thus, the moderate nationalists in this context evoked the idea of many perspectives in history, yet the national perspective was still superior for them. As the first quote suggested, the moderate nationalists were concerned that the textbooks do not show the peasant roots of the Polish nation properly. The second quote also indicates the dominance of the national perspective. The quoted teachers criticised the description of the social issue in terms of the national framework, which shows that it was the partitioners who oppressed the peasants. At the same time, however, he himself reproduced a nationalist interpretation of history, saying that the partitioners did not oppress the peasants but that there was a conflict between Poles and

Poles, not taking into account the interpretation of history that demonstrates that peasants in the 19th century generally did not consider themselves to be Polish because they did not think in national terms. The moderate nationalists were more critical of the textbooks than the conformists, but in one respect they resembled them. They were interested in the peasant issue only as an element of the emergence of the modern Polish nation. In other words, they talked about peasants in the context of the process of their full integration into the Polish nation, which was duly delayed in their opinion by the egoism of the upper classes.

Secondly, the moderate nationalists in the context of class and class conflict also focused on the industrial revolution and workers' rights. They talked about issues of economic and social inequality, the living conditions of workers and workers' children, the emergence of trade unions, and workers' fight for their rights. The most interested in these topics were teachers who came from and worked in the regions of Poland with a long industrial tradition and a history of workers' movements. For those teachers, economic and social history was important because it was local history that resonates with the living memory of local inhabitants:

> It's very clear during the industrial revolution that there are rich factory owners and those poor workers who work 18 hours a day without any, I don't know, health insurance; here it's shown very well, there's the hard situation of the worker, and the factory owners, and then the fight of these workers, the trade unions, it is shown how the trade unions were created.

Interestingly, teachers who were teaching in predominantly agricultural regions with a long history of serfdom (in central and eastern regions of present-day Poland, it lasted until the 1870s) usually did not underline the peasant past and did not draw on local memories, reflecting the aforementioned silencing of the peasants' experiences in the Polish collective memory as if it was some kind of social taboo. In conclusion, the moderate nationalists argued that class inequality was an important topic but only in the past. By accepting or implicitly reproducing the vision of linear progress, they asserted that, over time, the situation of subordinate groups has improved and class inequalities are fading away.

The issue of the social classes and class conflicts was stressed much more by the opponents, who criticised the textbooks for paying far too little attention to these issues:

> An intelligent student is able to draw the conclusion that inequalities existed from the very beginning, the division into social strata, into

different privileged groups, but that means there are no such direct themes, you have to search for them or the teacher will emphasize them in class.

The opponents believed that they had to introduce threads related to social classes and class conflicts themselves because they are marginalised in the textbooks. They focused mainly on peasants, and this reflects the left-wing attempts to restore the memory of the peasants' oppression in the early modern nobility's republic and to construct the Polish past from a people's history perspective. They stressed that the collective memory of peasants has been dominated by the nobility's experiences. As one of the teachers puts it, 'there're only noblemen, perhaps national minorities, but, for example, there're no peasants as some kind of historical actor'.

The opponents undermined the post-noble interpretation of the past in the spirit of critical history focusing on peasants' oppression, which in their opinion is neglected by the textbooks:

> We generally lack such an account of the whole history of the peasants' oppression in Poland and its significance for history; it has started a little bit in recent years, I suspect that before it goes to school, to school textbooks, it will still be a hundred years before it goes to schools.

They pointed out that the post-nobleman memory institutionalised by schools not only idealises the past but also has a strong impact on the identity of their pupils. In their opinion, the elimination of peasants' social history and their struggle from the school history education makes pupils unaware of their social background. In their opinion, education founded on the imaginations and narratives of the historically privileged group perpetuates the structures of class relations:

> Young people are deeply convinced that everyone is of the nobility . . . they're often very surprised when they realise that, statistically, 85% of their great-grandparents did their serfdom work and that this is what a historian should talk about . . . we've to fight this elitism, which is misunderstood, because why are the young people credited with having wealthy parents? . . . I think that emphasising these inequalities . . . that we've so much to do at the moment, precisely when it comes to restoring a proper place to peasants in Polish history, because it's the case that our history is the history of several hundred magnates, the nobility . . . we need to focus on this, and, unfortunately, I don't think we have much room for history to talk about other inequalities. We talk

about class and nationality, and I think we have to leave the issue of gender and sexual inequality behind for the time being.

The quote shows that the opponents were not a homogeneous group: they differed in the importance that they attached to various inequalities. Some focused on gender inequalities; others, like the aforementioned teacher, pointed out primarily class differences. Nevertheless, what is important is that the opponents placed the issue of class inequality in the context of a broader problem of understanding history as a discourse that is part of the cultural hegemony. Two issues are important in this context.

Firstly, the opponents challenged the hegemonic discourse, presenting the lower classes as being deprived of agency. They often deliberately engaged in the creation of counter-memory by referring to history from below and the concept of people's history and showing the perspectives of groups that were traditionally excluded from mainstream historiography, such as peasants:

> What is very important is the issue of the agency of the lower classes . . . to put it in Gramscian terms . . . if there's mention of, for example, revolts . . . actually all peasant revolts are presented as obviously lost . . . and as far as Poland is concerned, for example, the partitions . . . it's again a peasant issue . . . abolishing servitude, the abolition of serfdom, enfranchisement. . . . it's presented in such a convention that there are elites who discussed how to enfranchise the people, and there are people who were passive . . . the people are something that is talked about, not something that has an agency in these textbooks.

The second aspect of their approach to the issue of class social inequalities is the problematisation of liberal historiosophy and the contestation, in contrast to moderate nationalists, of the claim that class inequalities are an important topic but only in the context of the past. The interviewees, therefore, criticised the idea of linear progress based on the assumption that, over time, the situation of subordinate groups improves and class inequalities decrease:

> There's such a wandering model . . . such a liberal model . . . inequalities are sometimes presented as such a mistake in the past, yes, in the end they'd be equalised at some point in future . . . those groups that had been worse off, they would emancipate one way or another . . . these textbooks do not really talk, for example . . . they talk about trade unions in the 19th century or about strikes, or even about socialists and

communists . . . but I don't think they can tell us so clearly that we owe them the free weekends and the eight-hour working day; yes, rather if they do, it's in the convention that it used to be that way, and now it's different because it has changed.

The opponents aimed to explain to their students that historical processes have their contemporary consequences and to demonstrate that the changes were not made by themselves or were not only the work of the elite but also the result of the actions of people who were excluded from the dominant historical discourse. When talking about social inequalities and social classes, the opponents often took a committed approach close to that of critical history. They challenged the dominant narrative and used history to make students aware of the existence of inequalities in the past as well as in the modern world. However, the opponents wanted less to replace schools' dominant narrative with another supposedly better and true one and more to sensitise pupils, especially in secondary schools, to the existence of different perspectives on the past. They declared that they used constructivist methods and left students a great deal of freedom to interpret the past, encouraging them to work on their own and to reflect on the political entanglement of history.

Conclusions

In this chapter, we focused our analysis on the way in which the teachers approach the issue of representation of the non-European world as well as selected disadvantaged groups – national minorities, women, and the lower social classes – which have traditionally been marginalised in school history. Our analyses show that, in the context of the representation of the non-European world, the radical nationalists, conformists, and moderate nationalists reproduced hegemonic notions. They focused mainly on European history and perceived the non-European world in terms of Orientalist discourse or a clash of civilisations. This does not mean that there were no differences between them: the radical nationalists were more likely to refer to the discourse of the clash of civilisations, especially in the context of Islam. There were greater differences between the three categories taught when it came to the issues of minorities, women, and the lower classes. The radical nationalists and conformists reproduced a hegemonic narrative excluding minorities and women. Paradoxically, although the radical nationalists often had right-wing sympathies, their vision of history had nothing to do with right-wing populism since they focused on the elites. The moderate nationalists took a negotiated position. On the one hand, they challenged many elements of the hegemonic historical narrative, such as the

Whose nation? Whose history? 85

stereotype of a Catholic Pole, the small number of women in textbooks, or the lack of emphasis on inequality. One could say that they referred to a critical history. On the other hand, it was a Polonocentric history in which the place of women, minorities, or lower classes was limited and presented as objective and true. At the other extreme, there were opponents who not only questioned the content of the textbooks but also believed that the whole concept of history on which school teaching is based must be rethought in the spirit of a disciplinary approach.

References

Anderson, B. (1991). *Imagined communities: Reflections on the origin and spread of nationalism*. London: Verso.
Assmann, A. (2011). *Cultural memory and Western civilization: Functions, media, archives*. New York: Cambridge University Press.
Balogun, B. (2018). Polish lebensraum: The colonial ambition to expand on racial terms. *Ethnic and Racial Studies, 41*(3), 1–19.
Balogun, B. (2020). Race and racism in Poland: Theorising and contextualising 'Polish-centrism'. *Sociological Review, 68*, 1196–1211.
Bobako, M. (2017). *Islamofobia jako technologia władzy. Studium z antropologii politycznej [Islamophobia as a technology of power: A study in political anthropology]*. Kraków: Universitas.
Bryan, A. (2009). The intersectionality of nationalism and multiculturalism in the Irish curriculum: Teaching against racism? *Race, Ethnicity and Education, 12*, 297–317.
Burszta, W. J., Dobrosielski, P., Jaskulowski, K., Majbroda, K., Majewski, P., & Rauszer, M. (2019). *Naród w szkole: Historia i nacjonalizm w polskiej edukacji szkolnej [The nation at school: History and nationalism in Polish school education]*. Gdańsk: Katedra.
Connell, R. W. (2005). *Masculinities*. Berkeley: University of California Press.
Davies, N. (1997). Polish national mythologies. In G. Hosking & G. Schoepflin (Eds.), *Myths and nationhood* (pp. 141–157). New York: Routledge.
Dobrosielski, P. (2017). *Spory o Grossa. Polskie problemy z pamięcią o Żydach [Disputes about gross. Polish problems with the memory of Jews]*. Warsaw: IBL PAN.
Fish, S. (1997). Boutique multiculturalism, or why liberals are incapable of thinking about hate speech. *Critical Inquiry, 23*, 378–395.
Górak-Sosnowska, K., & Pachocka, M. (2019). Islamophobia and the quest for European identity in Poland. In I. Zempi & I. Awan (Eds.), *The Routledge international handbook of islamophobia* (pp. 225–236). London: Routledge.
Hall, S. (1992). The west and the rest. In S. Hall & B. Gieben (Eds.), *Formations of modernity* (pp. 275–331). Cambridge: Polity Press.
Huntington, S. P. (2011). *The clash of civilizations and the remaking of world order*. New York: Simon & Schuster.
Hutchins, R. D. (2016). *Nationalism and history education: Curricula and textbook in the United States and France*. New York: Routledge.

Jaskulowski, K. (2012). *Wspolnota symboliczna [Symbolic community]*. Gdansk: Katedra.
Jaskulowski, K. (2019). *The everyday politics of migration crisis in Poland: Between nationalism, fear and empathy*. Cham: Palgrave.
Jaskulowski, K., & Majewski, P. (2020). Politics of memory in upper Silesian schools: Between Polish homogeneous nationalism and its Silesian discontents. *Memory Studies, 13*(1), 60–73.
Jaskulowski, K., & Surmiak, A. (2017). Teaching history, teaching nationalism: A qualitative study of history teachers in a Polish post-industrial town. *Critical Studies in Education, 58*, 36–51.
Kalicińska J. (2011). Obraz kontynentów pozaeuropejskich w polskich podręcznikach do nauczania historii [The image of non-European continents in Polish history textbooks]. *Znaczenia, 5*, 163–178.
Kurczewska, J. (1999). Pierwsi nacjonaliści polscy i sprawy kobiet [First Polish nationalist and women's questions]. *Archiwum Historii Filozofii i Myśli Społecznej, 44*, 191–201.
Leszczyński, A. (2020). *Ludowa historia Polski [People's history of Poland]*. Warszawa: WAB.
Łodziński, S. (2005). *Równość i różnica. Mniejszości narodowe w porządku demokratycznym w Polsce po 1989 r [Equality and difference: National minorities in democratic Poland after 1989]*. Warszawa: Scholar.
Markiewka, T. (2017). *Język neoliberalizmu: Filozofia, polityka i media [The language of neoliberalism: Philosophy, politics and media]*. Toruń: UMK.
Mosse, G. L. (1988). *Nationalism and sexuality: Middle-class morality and sexual norms in modern Europe*. Madison: University of Wisconsin Press.
Motyka, G. (2011). *Od rzezi wołyńskiej do akcji Wisła [From Volyn massacre to action Vistula]*. Kraków: Wydawnictwo Literackie.
Nagel, J. (1998). Masculinity and nationalism: Gender and sexuality in the making of nations. *Ethnic and Racial Studies, 21*, 242–269.
Pędziwiatr, K. (2017). Islamophobia in Poland. National report 2016. In E. Bayraklı & F. Hafez, *European islamophobia report 2016* (pp. 413–438). Istanbul: SETA.
Rauszer, M. (2020). *Bękarty pańszczyzny [Inglourious basterds of serfdom]*. Warszawa: RM.
Rüssen, J. (2004). Historical consciousness: Narrative structure, moral function and ontogenetic development. In P. Seixas (Ed.), *Theorizing historical consciousness* (pp. 63–85). Toronto: Toronto University Press.
Said, E. (1978). *Orientalism*. London: Routledge and Kegan Paul.
Stradling, R. (2003). *Multiperspectivity in history teaching: A guide for teachers*. Strasburg: Council of Europe.
Szwed, A., & Zielińska, K. (2017). A war on gender? The roman catholic church's discourse on gender in Poland. In S. Ramet & I. Borowik (Eds.), *Religion, politics, and values in Poland* (pp. 113–136). New York: Palgrave.
Van Nieuwenhuyse, K. (2019). Empire and imperialism in education since 1945: Secondary school history textbooks. In I. Ness & Z. Cope (Eds.), *The Palgrave encyclopaedia of imperialism and anti-imperialism* (pp. 1–15). Cham: Palgrave.

Van Nieuwenhuyse, K., & Valentim, J. P. (Eds.). (2018). *The colonial past in history textbooks: Historical and social psychological perspectives.* Charlotte, NC: Information Age Publishing.

Walczewska, S. (2000). *Damy, rycerze i feministki [Ladies, knights and feminists].* Warszawa: Efka.

Wallerstein, I. (2006). *European universalism: The rhetoric of power.* New York: New Press.

Wansik, B., Akkerman, S., Zuiker, I., & Wubbels, T. (2018). Where does teaching multiperspectivity in history education begin and end? An analysis of the uses of temporality. *Theory & Research in Social Education, 48,* 495–527.

Woźniczka, Z. (2010). *Represje Na Górnym Śląsku Po 1945 Roku [Repression in Upper Silesia after 1945].* Katowice: Śląsk.

Yuval-Davis, N., & Anthias, F. (Eds.). (1989). *Woman, nation, state.* Houndmills: Macmillan Press.

6 What next for teaching history?

In the book, we investigated why teachers think it is worth teaching history at school. We distinguished four types of teachers: radical nationalists, who considered the core curriculum to be not 'patriotic' enough and completely subordinated education to nationalist goals; conformists, with a passive approach and acceptance of the core curriculum and textbooks, who took the nationalist functions of history for granted; moderate nationalists, who combined the nationalist education model with the civic model; and the opponents, who contested nationalist history teaching model. Despite the differences between the first three types of teachers, they all shared the conviction that school history should be content focused and should aim to nationalise pupils. Briefly, the aim of school history education is to instil in students a canonical story about the Polish nation, which is intended to form the basis of their collective identity. The teachers assigned history a nationalising function and, at the same time, were convinced that history is an objective science (which in itself is questionable). From the perspective of the teachers' subjective rationality, this was not a contradiction because they believed that history is simply the history of nations that exist as objective and real social beings and are not a corollary of nationalist discourse. The fourth type, a small group of the opponents, believed that the aim of school history is primarily to teach history as a discipline, although elements of critical history also appeared in their approach. They gave priority to cognitive goals, believing that schools should not teach nationalism but include it as one of many ideologies of the modern period.

This book speaks of the dominance of the nationalist model of education in Poland. The core curriculum and textbooks defined the objectives of education in nationalist categories, and, for most of the teachers, the nationalisation of students is an obvious goal of school education, not counting a small group of the opponents. However, while the teachers agreed on the nationalising function of history, there were also differences between them. We focused on two main problems, namely the type of nationalism

DOI: 10.4324/9781003028529-6

that teachers promote when teaching history and the kind of history that they teach in the context of selected disadvantaged groups, such as women, minorities, lower social classes, and the non-European world. We showed that teachers differ in their understanding of national belonging (exclusive versus inclusive), the extent to which they focus on the Polish nation (Poland first versus international nationalism), how they understand duties towards the nation (militarist versus mundane nationalism), and the extent to which they discuss the dark sides of national history (celebratory versus critical nationalism). Although it is not possible to assign types of nationalism unequivocally to particular categories of teachers, one can discern some tendencies: the radical nationalists tended to refer to closed, exclusive, militaristic, and glorifying nationalism, while the moderate nationalists were more inclined to refer to open, international, mundane, and critical nationalism.

The teachers also displayed various understandings of the canonical history of the Polish nation. We analysed the differences in their approach to the non-European world, indicating the dominance of discourses on Orientalism and the clash of civilisations. We also showed the differences between teachers with regard to their attitude towards national minorities, women, and lower classes. The radical nationalists, in accordance with the logic of exclusionary nationalism, did not leave much room for minorities. They also defined history as the history of men for men: a collection of male heroes who should serve as role models for male pupils. They avoided talking about class conflicts and inequality. Although they had right-wing sympathies, there was no right-wing populism, referring to the conflict between the elite and the people, in their approach to history. The moderate nationalists were more critical of the textbooks; for example, they argued that there should be more topics about minorities or women. One could say that they aimed to develop critical historical consciousness among pupils. They used history, for example, to undermine certain elements of hegemonic Polishness, such as the auto-stereotype of a Catholic Pole. However, their treatment of history was still based on a traditional concept focused on the Polish nation and on political history and men's achievements. They applied a critical approach to questioning hegemonic history but not their own narrative. The opponents, however, argued that the problem was not so much the number of topics devoted to women or minorities but the very concept of school history itself, which was based on narrowly understood political history. The opponents believed that history should be taught as a discipline, which means not just working with historical sources but, above all, also trying to explain to pupils how historical knowledge is produced and how it is conditioned and positioned. The opponents did not want simply to replace one narrative with another better one but believed that students should be taught how to conduct critical analysis on their own and to create their own historical narratives.

In the light of our findings, there is no confirmation of the assumption of right-wing education reform, which we mentioned in the first chapter. Let us recall that Beata Szydło's right-wing government carried out the reform in 2017. The government framed historical education as being in a state of crisis, that is, as not playing a nationalising function, which gave it the motivation to introduce a reform strengthening the nationalist education model. As the commentary on the new core curriculum for PSs explained, 'The essence of the changes in the history teaching in the new core curriculum is the emphasis on the educational, patriotic and emotional aspects, which will influence building national consciousness and historical identity' (MEN, 2018a, p. 26). As we also read in the commentary:

> Arousing love for our motherland will be possible through learning about the history of our nation, its achievements, its mother tongue, as well as characters whose achievements have permanently determined our history . . . general history will remain an important aspect, but it should be treated as a background. . . . The pupils' emotional attitude towards their motherland history should be developed already during the first history lessons in the 4th grade. This will be done by looking at the distant and closer past through the prism of figures of great importance for the shaping of Polish cultural identity. . . . The choice of characters is determined by the course of Polish history which is defined by the defence of identity, faithfulness to principles and beliefs, attachment to our own sovereign state.
>
> (MEN, 2018a, pp. 23–24)

Thus, the main aim of the reform is to awaken love for the nation. Before children begin to understand history, an emotional attitude towards the nation should be developed through the celebration of national figures (male by default). At the same time, it is claimed that the list of these national heroes is imposed by history itself. It is assumed that the catalogue of characters is not conditioned by a nationalist understanding of history but reflects the objective structure of the past. The new core curriculum promotes a model for teaching history that is subordinated to nationalist goals but, at the same time, assumes that history has an objective character. Pupils are to familiarise themselves with the canonical narration of the past, which is presented as objective. The main element of this past is the Polish nation represented by historical figures who defended its identity and sovereignty, with whom pupils should emotionally identify themselves. History, understood as discipline, is relegated to the background:

> A pupil leaving primary school will know that it is impossible to build a future without a historical memory – a memory rooted in the past. In the previous core curriculum, these issues were in the background. More attention was paid to historical chronology, historical analysis and interpretation and the construction of narrative.
> (MEN, 2018a, p. 24)

Similar objectives are set by the core curriculum for secondary education, which also emphasises that 'historical education has important pedagogical objectives'. These pedagogical goals include 'strengthening the sense of love for the Motherland through respect and attachment to the tradition and history of our own nation and its achievements, culture and mother tongue'. As we read further, 'building ties with the home country, civic awareness, an attitude of respect and responsibility for our own state; strengthening the sense of national dignity and pride; building respect for other people and for the achievements of other nations and countries'. Although there are more topics on general history in UPSs than in PSs, 'obviously, the theme of the homeland history remains the most important' (MEN, 2018b, p. 11).

This book shows that, contrary to right-wing rhetoric, the reform was not a rupture but a radicalisation of the current practice of history teaching, which has dangerous consequences for history education. Firstly, the reform institutionalises exclusionary, celebratory, and uncritical nationalism, and it seems to correspond to the views of the radical nationalists whom we analysed. The PiS reform radicalises the existing trends by not only institutionalising the nationalist model of teaching history but also strengthening the position of the radical nationalists in the educational system. The radical nationalists not only prioritised nationalist aims over cognitive ones but also tended to define the Polish nation in exclusionary terms, advocating Poland first nationalism and uncritical nationalism focused on content-related history taught by celebrating male national heroes. This type of nationalism is not compatible with contemporary Polish society, which is becoming increasingly diverse in many respects. For example, more and more migrants are coming to Poland, new forms of family life are emerging that differ from the so-called traditional family, attachment to institutional religions is decreasing and new forms of religious or spiritual movements are gaining in popularity, and gender roles are changing and women are striving for greater equality and inclusion. The reform subordinates education to the right-wing vision of society and strengthens its hegemony in Polish society. It does not take into account that male heterosexual ethnic Catholic Poles do not constitute the Polish nation but are just one of the many groups that make up the diverse Polish nation, all of which have their own history, experiences, and memories.

While this threat of right-wing hegemony is not convincing for everyone, the second threat should also concern those who do not share our political views. Historical education in Poland is heading towards a model of teaching that shapes naive historical thinking, which does not make it possible to understand what historical knowledge is or what role history plays in society. The reform strengthens the tendency to focus on content-related historical knowledge and on teaching students a coherent story about the past, which is supposed to have an identitary function. Pupils are to remember the key dates and names of national heroes and to understand history as a one-line process from Mieszko I to the contemporary Polish nation state. They are to identify themselves emotionally with this canonical story because it explains to them where they come from and what their roots and responsibilities are. In the light of the new reforms, such issues as teaching students historical methods or making students understand the nature of historical knowledge are much less important than instilling in them a love for their homeland and pride in their nation. In other words, the reform places little emphasis on developing knowledge about the knowledge of the past. Such an approach would require the development of genetic historical thinking, that is, the ability to engage in contextual reading and evaluation of the validity of historical evidence and to understand that history is not a complete, coherent story but a continuous process of constructing and reconstructing knowledge that will always be incomplete and partial because it refers to fragmented and random historical sources, which are full of gaps, inconsistencies, and prejudices, and that it is susceptible to political and ideological positioning (Rüssen, 2004; Wineburg, 2018). For the vast majority of pupils, school is the only place where they can acquire knowledge about knowledge of the past, that is, about history as a discipline. Without this metahistorical knowledge, they will remain naive recipients of historical content and consumers of memory, unable to assess its reliability and social and political functions, and susceptible to various forms of manipulation.

References

MEN. (2018a). *Podstawa programowa kształcenia ogólnego z komentarzem: szkoła podstawowa historia – historia [Core curriculum for general education with commentary: Primary school – history]*. Warszawa: MEN.

MEN. (2018b). *Podstawa programowa kształcenia ogólnego z komentarzem: szkoła ponadpodstawowa – historia [Core curriculum for general education with commentary: Secondary school – history]*. Warszawa: MEN.

Rüssen, J. (2004). Historical consciousness: Narrative structure, moral function and ontogenetic development. In P. Seixas (Ed.), *Theorizing historical consciousness* (pp. 63–85). Toronto: Toronto University Press.

Wineburg, S. (2018). *Why learn history (when it's already on your phone)*. Chicago and London: The University of Chicago Press.

Index

Africa 58–59
anti-Semitism 64–65, 70
Asia 21, 48

Battle of Grunwald 35, 68–69
Belarusians 21
Billig, M. 10, 11, 31, 34
Boykos 64
Brubaker, R. 11
Bruner, J. S. 14

Catholicism 21, 44
Christianity 33, 44
civic model of education 15–16, 31, 40, 88
civic nationalism 42–43
collective memory, definition 12–13
colonialism 59–60
communism 17, 32, 56
constructivism 9–11, 23–24
cursed soldiers 32, 34, 51–52, 54, 71

disciplinary model of education 15, 38, 40, 76, 85
Durkheim, E. 10

ethnic nationalism 42–43
ethnosymbolism 10
Europe 31, 33, 46, 47, 48, 51, 58–62, 65, 73, 75, 84
European Union 53, 62

Fascist Italy 78
First World War 14

Germans 31, 31, 63, 65, 68, 69
Germany 15, 46, 47, 51, 61, 68
Giertych, R. 45
Gross, J.T. 63

Hall, S. 11, 13
hegemony 12, 13, 83, 92

integral nationalism 21, 50
Islam 61, 62, 84
Islamophobia 61, 62

Jews 21, 63–66, 70

Kansteiner, W. 12
Katyń massacre 17

Lady of Czestochowa 72
Lemkos 64
Lévesque, S. 13
Lithuanians 35

Marx, K. 13
Marxism 37, 76, 77, 79, 80
masculinity 71, 74
Ministry of National Education 11, 13, 17, 19, 20
modernism 9–10
modernity 60, 61
Muslims 61–62

National Day of the Cursed Soldiers 52
nationalism, definition 11
nationalist model of education 15–16, 23, 29, 36, 37, 40
Nazi Germany 69, 78
neoliberalism 77, 79
nobility 71, 78–80, 82
North America 45, 58

Orientalism 5, 36, 58, 59, 60, 84, 89

Yang, Y. 2006. *Whispers and Moans: Interviews with the Men and Women of Hong Kong's Sex Industry*. Hong Kong: Blacksmith.

Yee, Gale A. and Y.H. Yieh, eds. 2016. *Honoring the Past, Looking to the Future: Essays from the 2014 International Congress of the Ethnic Chinese Biblical Scholars*. Hong Kong: Divinity School of Chung Chi College, The Chinese University of Hong Kong.

Yip, Wing Man. 2014. "Don't Be So Quick to Condemn 'Immoral' Young Sex Workers". *South China Morning Post*, 12 December. Retrieved from: www.scmp.com/comment/insight-opinion/article/1661371/dont-be-so-quick-condemn-immoral-young-sex-workers.

Subjects and authors index

#MeToo 20, 26, 28n23, 28n25

abused/abusers 3, 9–10, 13, 15, 20, 25–6, 28n16, 39, 41, 43, 49, 54, 61, 65, 68, 77–9, 81, 83, 87–8
abusiveness 23, 41, 65, 68, 75, 77–8, 84, 90
Adullam/Adullamite 31, 35
adultery 11n7, 36, 55, 72, 80; adulteress 48, 69, 71, 73–4, 80–1, 83, 86–7, 89
AFRO 21–3
Amnesty International 25, 53–4, 60–1
assault/assaulted 28n16, 54; indecent assault 4, 14–16; sexual assault 14–16, 18

Bible 3–5, 8–10, 26, 31, 34, 39, 41, 46, 54, 56–7, 59, 63, 68, 70, 75, 77, 79–80, 87, 90
biblical: authors 5, 8, 34, 36, 48, 62–3, 76, 80, 83; interpreters 4–5, 76, 88–90; *see also* commentators; interpretation
Bird, Phyllis 46, 52n35, 85n22
body/bodies 6, 18, 20, 25, 34–5, 41–2, 44–5, 51n28, 59, 68, 70, 75–6, 87, 89
bullying 10, 26, 36, 89

Camp, Claudia 64
child 35, 37, 55, 57–9, 65; childless/childlessness 31, 33, 40; children 41, 60, 63, 82, 88, 89; of Gomer's 69, 71–7, 79; of sex workers 10, 26, 44–5, 60, 63, 77–9, 81, 84, 86, 90
Chinese Christianity 8, 12n20; *see also* Christian

Chiu, Andrew 32–6, 40, 42
Christian/s 12n20, 19, 22, 47, 49, 31–2, 36, 47, 49, 70, 73, 78, 80, 86–7, 89, 90; Chinese 32–3, 37, 78; of Hong Kong 22, 32, 36, 56, 70, 87; as interpretation/s 10, 32, 36, 56, 70; as interpreters 68; as non-Christians 47; as readers 10, 90; *see also* commentator; interpretation
Church/church 9, 12n20, 18–21, 23 28n22, 86
clients 11n6, 17, 23, 25–6, 38–9, 43, 48, 61, 65, 68, 75, 81–2, 87–8
commentary 9, 32–3, 37, 39, 42, 47, 56, 66n25, 70, 75, 79, 86–7
commentators (biblical) 5, 36, 39–42, 45, 47, 56–8, 63–4, 70–1, 77, 81–2
consent/consenting 3–4, 14–15, 17, 20, 28n17, 38, 87–8; non-consent 17, 61
crimes 1–4, 7, 11n6, 13–15, 24, 26, 36, 40, 54, 59, 61, 86–8; as hate crimes 10; as sexual 11n6, 13, 15, 19–20, 26
criminal 2, 4, 25
criminalise/criminalised/criminalising (sex work) 5, 7–8, 25, 59, 65; criminalization 7

daughters 31, 34, 41, 50–1n28, 53, 64, 69; as daughter-in-law 33, 35, 39, 43
decriminalise/decriminalised/decriminalising 7, 25, 87

fathers 31–3, 41, 50–1n28, 54–5, 77, 82, 88; as father-in-law 35
females 1, 5, 8, 11n7, 13–15, 18, 20–2, 29n39, 35–6, 46–8, 51n28, 61, 63–4,

patriotism 30–31, 33, 37, 54, 67, 78
peasants 78–83
Piast myth 17
Piłsudski, J. 44
Pole-Catholic 63, 65, 66
primordialism 10

racism 59
Russia 46, 49, 54, 55, 65, 69
Russians 31, 52, 63

Second World War 21, 54, 69, 70
Seixas, P. 2, 15
serfdom 81–83

Tatars 35
Turks 35

Ukrainians 21, 31, 63, 64, 66
Upper Silesia 22, 47, 67–70
Upper Silesian Civil War 68–69
Upper Silesian Tragedy 68

Van Nieuwenhuyse, K. 15

Wallerstein, I. 61
Warsaw Uprising 47, 74
Weber, M. 15, 55
West 45, 60, 75
Wielkopolska Uprising 67
Williams, G.A. 11
Wojdon, J. 19, 20, 37
women 3, 5, 22, 58, 62, 70–76, 84–85, 89, 91
working class 17, 79, 81

For Product Safety Concerns and Information please contact our EU representative GPSR@taylorandfrancis.com
Taylor & Francis Verlag GmbH, Kaufingerstraße 24, 80331 München, Germany

www.ingramcontent.com/pod-product-compliance
Lightning Source LLC
Chambersburg PA
CBHW051758230426
43670CB00012B/2338